PEAK PERFORMANCE PRINCIPLES FOR HIGH ACHIEVERS

JOHN R. NOE is a well-known member of the National Speakers Association and was chosen as one of the seventeen top speakers in the United States and Canada to be featured in the book *Star Spangled Speakers*. He has climbed mountains all over the world, including the Matterhorn, Mt. Kilimanjaro and Grand Teton. Noe is president of IMH Systems in Indianapolis, Indiana, and directs seminars which train and inspire non-mountain climbers to reach great heights in their own lives. An active Christian, Noe lives with his wife and two children in Indianapolis.

PEAK PERFORMANCE PRINCIPLES FOR HIGH ACHIEVERS is Noe's dramatic true story of how he transformed himself, sedentary and out-of-shape in his mid-thirties, into the dynamic leader he is today—and how you can too.

Berkley books by John R. Noe

Peak Performance Principles for High Achievers
People Power

Peak Performance Principles For High Achievers

JOHN R. NOE

BERKLEY BOOKS, NEW YORK

Grateful acknowledgment is given for permission to reprint the following:

Poems on page 36 from *A Pictorial Life of Jack London*, Russ Kingman, New York: The Crown Publishing Group. Excerpts on pages 178-179 from *Have You Heard of the Four Spiritual Laws?* Copyright © Campus Crusade for Christ, Inc., 1965. All rights reserved.

This Berkley book contains the complete
text of the original hardcover edition.
It has been completely reset in a typeface
designed for easy reading and was printed
from new film.

PEAK PERFORMANCE PRINCIPLES FOR HIGH ACHIEVERS

A Berkley Book / published by arrangement with
Frederick Fell Publishers, Inc.

PRINTING HISTORY
Frederick Fell edition published 1984
Berkley edition / January 1986

ISBN: 0-425-10150-9

A BERKLEY BOOK ® TM 757,375
Berkley Books are published by The Berkley Publishing Group,
200 Madison Avenue, New York, New York 10016.
The name "BERKLEY" and the "B" logo
are trademarks belonging to Berkley Publishing Corporation.

PRINTED IN THE UNITED STATES OF AMERICA

20   19   18   17   16   15   14   13

Acknowledgments

Every high achievement in my life has been accomplished under the expert guidance of valuable and talented people, and the writing of this book is no exception. While it would be impossible to acknowledge everyone, there are a few people who have acted as my expert guides and I would like to express my gratitude to them.

I am indebted to my parents, who patiently and religiously endured my reckless years and taught me the value of work and effort. I would like to give my tender thanks to Roseman Pittman, who tutored me through the second and third grades when I was falling behind my classmates. My first role-model manager, Rod Stephens, I thank for giving me great opportunities to see the world and to pattern my management style after his example. I thank John Volpalensky for all the hours he invested as we wrestled with difficulties, disappointments, and discouragements in starting my first business. It was only his inexhaustible enthusiasm and humorous exaggerations that saved me from defeat. I am grateful to my mountain-climbing guides: Alfons Franzen, who took me to the top of the Matterhorn; and Moses and Good Luck for safely leading my wife and me up Mount Kilimanjaro. I would like to thank my fellow speaker and confidante, Nido Qubein, whose advice, help, and confidence in me and the Peak Performance Principles were vitally important in furthering my personal and professional life, as well as in furthering my company's management expertise. I would like to extend special thanks to Ralph Walls, D.D.S., for opening my eyes to the Lord, teaching me how to live a richer and fuller life, and ensuring that I will spend eternity in heaven with the Lord Jesus Christ. I am also grateful to my brother Jim, whose life has blossomed and now blesses many other lives including my own.

I thank all the high achievers who work with our company and who believe in the sources of motivation and service that must be applied for peak performance. Without their contribution I could not have enjoyed the experiences I have described in this book. In turn, I am also grateful to the individuals and corporations who have engaged our company to train, educate, and develop their personnel toward higher achievement.

My greatest debt, however, is to my wife Cindy and to our children, Elise and Ken. Each was a gift from God for which I thank Him every day. They have taught me the joy of high achievement in my areas of responsibility as a husband and father. They give me strength and courage, as well as the ability to keep my priorities on a straight path.

To all of you, please accept this book as a token of my deepest thanks. God bless you, have a good climb in your life, and may you climb from peak to peak to The Peak in heaven.

To my loving wife Cindy, who continually amazes me with her energy and high achievements as a wife, mother, business partner, and child of God.

Contents

Preface

No, I never started out to write a book. Originally, I planned simply to describe the details of my mountain climbs to any church or business group that might ask me to speak. However, as I began speaking, many of the people in my audiences became more interested in the motivational and inspirational messages behind my descriptions than in the descriptions themselves. Because of this, I decided to change the emphasis of my presentations from mountain-climbing descriptions to how each individual in the audience could use the climbing principles, ideas, and techniques to reach greater heights in their own lives—heights they never dreamed possible.

I have written this book to provide a lasting source of inspiration and guidance for readers wishing to become high achievers. In a straightforward and easy-to-understand way, I have presented my ideas to help readers obtain their high goals. As you read this book, share with me the feelings and emotions of some of my high achievements. My examples should make the principles easier to identify with and motivate you to fulfill your dreams on your own.

If by the end of this book you realize that it doesn't take a superhuman to climb the great mountains of life or to achieve great heights of success, you will be well on your way toward becoming a peak performer. Enjoy the climb!

PART ONE

Do You Have What It Takes To Become a High Achiever?

The principles described in this book have come from my experiences climbing some of the world's greatest mountains—among them the Matterhorn in Switzerland and Kilimanjaro in Africa. You are invited to come along with me as I relive some of those climbs: to share my feelings, emotions, doubts, and thrills. It's your opportunity to learn about these experiences without the torture of brutal physical exertion and mental anguish.

Caution: The ideas in this book are hazardous to your complacency and self-satisfaction. They can produce symptoms such as dissatisfaction with traditional definitions of success, an overwhelming urge to break away from a mundane existence, and a compelling drive to be all God created you to be in every dimension of your life.

You might discover, as I did, that even though your life looks full—although you have a good act going— there is a nagging emptiness, a vague sense that there is something more than what you have found so far. You may feel a deep urge to expand your horizons, to pursue all that life offers, to embark on a lifetime of high goals and achievement.

But I must warn you—climbing life's mountains is a risky business. It will mean saying no to false values, the ones that always drive you to build your security through conformity. It will mean overcoming your pain thresholds and entering a dimension where your will is more important than your emotions. It will mean abandoning all illusions of your false self and searching for your authentic existence.

You can make it, but it will take all you've got. If you're willing to take the risk to become all you are, read on. This first section will help you answer the question, Do you have what it takes to become a high achiever?

1

The "Classic" Mountain

The Matterhorn casts an uncanny spell over the tiny village of Zermatt, Switzerland. She towers majestically over the lesser Alpine peaks, attracting tourists and mountaineers from all around the world. She is indeed the most famous mountain in the world.

She's been called the "classic" mountain by thousands of skilled mountain climbers who've challenged her lofty peak during the last two centuries. Looking at her towering, craggy form, you can easily understand why she was the last of the major Alpine peaks conquered during the golden age of mountaineering in the late nineteenth century. It is no wonder that this massive obelisk, this "living rock" that looms at an altitude of 14,780 feet, has also been called the "Tiger of the Alps." You can imagine the eerie groans of the experienced climbers who've plummeted to their deaths from her treacherous ledges and shoulders. Don't do it! their timeless echoes whisper to the novices who come to try what others have died attempting.

3

But I knew I had to do it. There was to be no turning back now. For two years I had looked every day at a photograph in my den of the Matterhorn peak that inspired me to push my mind and body beyond their previous limits. That image—that *high goal*—led me to run every day until my body dropped in fatigue, to increase my mental and emotional boundaries close to their breaking points, to learn everything I could about mountain climbing.

I had worked my way back into top physical condition. I'd begun by running the block around my house, next moving on to complete the Indianapolis Mini-Marathon and then a full-scale marathon. I'd settled into a pattern of daily runs, which improved my lungs, my cardiovascular system, and my muscles. I was feeling better than I'd ever felt in my life. My mind was prepared also. I'd studied every available book and article on mountain climbing. Daily I practiced implementing intermediate goals that caused me to strengthen my alertness and deepen my commitment. Already I had begun to reap the benefits of a disciplined mind in my work, with my family, and in my spiritual development.

Technically I was ready as well. I'd practiced on the challenging slopes of the Grand Tetons in Wyoming and studied under some of the best mountain-climbing teachers in the world. I knew what I was doing.

And yet, I confess without embarrassment, fear gripped me as I faced the reality that I had only anticipated during those many years of preparation. Some say a picture is worth a thousand words. But, if that's true, reality is worth a thousand pictures. Everything about the Matterhorn is overpowering in proportion to all else.

I'd felt the tension building as I'd ridden for two hours on the cog-railway that winds through the steep mountain passes. I'd swallowed lump after lump that rose up in my throat as I had stood surveying the ominous, rocky form above me. The fear I felt was not so much a fear of death, but a haunting fear of failure. I'd seen the dejected looks on the faces of unsuccessful climbers who'd been waiting to reboard the little cog-railway car when I'd arrived, full of hope and excitement. I'd told all my friends, family, business associates, and audiences that I was going to climb the Matterhorn. If I failed how could I go home and face them?

But when fear knocked on the door, faith and confidence answered. In the deepest levels of my heart, I believed I could overcome my fear.

My First Priority

One of the most important principles that mountain climbing taught me is that you don't conquer fears by saying little clichés to yourself. You act. You take the first step toward your most immediate goal. In doing so, you make the crucial move from the position of fear into the arena of conflict. Then and only then can you get your mind and heart into what you are doing.

My first priority was to meet my guide. The Matterhorn is no mountain for an Indiana flatlander to treat casually. I had learned enough about mountain climbing to know that the most important step was to seek out an expert guide.

Alfons Franzen, a 6'2" German-speaking Swiss, was my choice. I'd learned about him from reading and asking questions, and I had specifically requested him. He'd consented to evaluate me and see what I could do before he would lead me to the top of the mountain of my dreams. When I shook his hand, it was firm. His steady eyes seemed to penetrate to the deepest regions of my soul as he sized me up. I knew I'd made the right choice—here was a man I could believe in, a person I could trust with my life and my dream.

But Alfons was not given to snap judgments. I thought I had seen a glimmer of approval in his eyes as he'd looked me over but, "We'll see," was all the commitment he was ready to make. Our lives and his reputation was on the line; he wasn't about to risk either on an American he didn't know.

I knew I'd have to prove myself before this man would trust me to follow him to the top of the Matterhorn. There would be a period of testing.

My Final Exam

Alfons and I hiked to the Riffelhorn the next day so that he could test my skills, conditioning, and attitudes. The Riffelhorn is the qualifying peak for all who dare to take on the Matterhorn. This was to be my final exam.

We climbed up and down the treacherous slopes and rocks of the Riffelhorn twice. Each step of the way, I marvelled at Alfons's deliberate moves and confidence. He was like an animal in his natural habitat. He watched my every move—the way I handled the rope, the way I placed my hands and feet, the way I followed directions. With cool detachment he evaluated everything I did and said. There was not the faintest clue in his voice or his eyes to let me know how I was doing.

Finally, late in the afternoon we finished the test. I waited for some indication as to whether I'd made it.

I dared not ask, for I had the feeling that it would be interpreted as a sign of weakness by this rugged, confident man of the mountains.

Slowly, he loosened the rope from my waist, let it fall, and stood looking me square in the eyes. I thought I saw a slight trace of a smile at the corners of his mouth.

"Well, John," he said at last, "it's going to be difficult for you, but I think we can make it *together*."

I'd qualified to climb the Matterhorn! Relatively few had made it even this far. Something told me the most difficult part was yet to come.

Was I Ready?

Our next step was to get into position to start the long two-day climb I'd awaited so long. A few days later, shortly after lunch, Alfons and I began the five-hour climb up the base of the Matterhorn to the 10,500-foot level, where a tiny hut clings tenaciously to the rock high above the glacier floor.

The last half mile of the climb grew increasingly steep, and required total concentration. Dinner was served at 7:30 P.M., and I was told to be in bed by 8:00. I'd be awakened at 3:00 the next morning to begin the next day's climb at 4:00.

After dinner, I stretched out on the bare mattress to try to get a good night's sleep. I knew that rest was essential because I'd need all my energy to make the exhausting climb the next day.

It was cold. Part of me wanted to be warm and comfortable, but part of me knew that the cold was an ally. The colder the temperature, the less danger there is that melting ice will dislodge rocks that can easily knock a climber off a tenuous footing, and the Matterhorn is notorious for falling rocks.

"Go to sleep!" I kept telling myself. The 3:00 A.M. wake-up call would come too quickly. It was crucial to get an early start on the climb so we could reach the top and be down off the peak before the sun rose high enough to start melting the surface ice and snow, loosening the rocks.

I felt like a high school athlete the night before a state championship game. My heart pounded as I stared at the stark wood ceiling in the dimly lit cabin. I was excited, scared, confident, proud, and humble, all at once. I knew I was where I should be, yet I marvelled that I was there. It was like riding an emotional roller coaster.

"Was I ready?" The nagging question kept repeating itself. Alfons thought I was, and I valued his judgment. I had thought I was ready, but now I was beginning to wonder if I should have trained longer or more vigorously. Everything I'd planned and worked so hard for during the last two years would be on the line tomorrow. I knew that if I contracted any severe symptoms of high-altitude sickness—dizziness, nausea, or a headache—Alfons would jerk me right off that mountain and we would abort the climb.

I felt trapped, caught in the middle. Above me lay the "Tiger," waiting to test my mettle, challenge my resolve, exploit my every weakness. Below me lay the yawning glacier floor, the people who loved me and believed in me, and the inevitable question: Did you make it?

How Did I Get Here?

Reason took over, and I began to see that it was too late for worrying. There was nothing I could do about any of the doubts now. Besides, I knew there was no turning back—my intuition told me I had to go for the ultimate.

I started recalling the long and arduous path that had led me to this moment of destiny. Like a videotape recorder, my mind searched through the events of the past and settled on a scene that had been stamped indelibly on my memory seven years earlier.

I was once again in the intensive care unit of a hospital. The room was a jungle of wires, tubes, and beeping, flashing devices. Nurses scurried about, checking vital life signs. Monitors sounded alarms, signaling flurries of frantic life-rescuing activity.

I hated it. I didn't want to be there. I didn't want anybody I loved to be in one of those sterile beds with all those levers and gadgets. Hospitals had always reminded me of suffering, pain, tragedy, and death.

A nurse led me to a bed in the far corner of the room where a body, covered with a white sheet, lay silent except for labored breathing. Tubes ran from the nostrils and the mouth. I looked down into the ashen face and saw a vaguely familiar form, but the lines were deeper, the eyes farther back into the head, the expression more fixed than I had remembered.

It was my father. He'd just undergone open-heart surgery—a triple by-pass operation. The arteries of his heart had become clogged by the sedentary chemistry of his body.

I loved him. I hurt for him. I wanted to jerk him out of that bed and make him well. But then, suddenly, another thought occurred to me—a far more personal and terrifying thought. "John," my family and friends had often said to me, "you're the spit'n' image of your father. You look just like him." The image of what I was quickly becoming—where I was heading—came crashing in upon me with full fury. I knew that if I remained tied to my desk, too busy making money and building a reputation for myself to develop both mind and body, I'd end up in the same condition as my father. I decided it was time to take seriously all those promises I'd been making myself for years. I knew that I was not only becoming a physical and mental "has-been"; I was becoming a physical and mental "never-will-be."

Yet, it was to be seven years before I began to make those promises become reality. The mental tape ran back to another, more recent scene.

I was sitting at my desk one day, looking at my deteriorating body. I was tired of being flabby and out of shape. I knew that my mental and managerial effectiveness would benefit if I were in good physical condition. So, without a lot of fanfare, I decided to do something about it. I knew I had to do it, *now*.

I Hadn't Planned To Be Here

"Funny," I thought almost aloud as I lay on that skimpy bare mattress in a small cabin two-thirds of the way to the top of the Matterhorn, "I hadn't really planned to be here—at least not at the beginning." My original goal was to get into good physical condition. I knew that the means I used had to be both lasting and fun.

For me, the answer was running long distances. My first goal was ridiculously mundane: It was simply to run all the way around the block on which I lived, a distance of only eight-tenths of a mile. But the first time I tried it, I couldn't do it. The second time I tried, I almost made it. But the third time I made it!

Over the next several months I continued to improve. Soon I could run a mile, then two miles, then five miles. Gradually, a strange phenomenon began to take place, a change that was crucial for what was to come in the future. As I reached new and greater distance goals in running, not only did I feel like I could do more, but I felt this surge of momentum that made me want to do more.

It's a pattern I now understand well—setting progressively higher intermediate goals and reaching them on schedule. It has become a way of life for me in my business, in my personal life, and with my family. In my seminars, it's one of the most important principles I present to people who want to become high achievers. You don't shoot for the moon with a Roman candle. You start with intermediate goals that are realistic and achievable. When you reach each intermediate goal, you set another, higher goal. It's the only way to build your confidence. Set goals that are too high, and you'll constantly feel the agony of defeat; set goals that are too low, and you'll never feel the ecstasy of great victory.

One day I ran six-and-a-half miles; that's half the distance of the Indianapolis Mini-Marathon. Then it dawned on me: If you can do half of something, you can do the whole thing. And I did it. In May of 1978, I entered the Indianapolis Mini-Marathon. I started downtown at Monument Circle, ran all the way to White River and out Sixteenth Street—on to the second turn of the Indianapolis Motor Speedway, around the third turn and the fourth turn. Finally, I ran across the finish line.

With improvement in running came improvement in my morale and confidence. I could feel my enthusiasm and confidence spreading to everything in my life.

After I'd run the Indianapolis Mini-Marathon, I went out and bought a two-by-three-foot picture of the Matterhorn and hung it in my den. But I wasn't setting the Matterhorn as a goal yet. After all, that was too big a step. It would have been ridiculous and foolhardy for me to challenge the world's greatest mountain at that time. What I needed were more intermediate goals that I could realistically tackle. So I developed a game plan to stretch my imagination, teach me the basic mountain-climbing skills I needed, and push me to a new level of physical fitness.

Later that summer my wife Cindy and I loaded our two children into the car and took off for the Grand Teton Mountains in Wyoming. There we entered mountain-climbing school. We learned techniques for fingerholds, toeholds, climbing up cracks and fissures, rappelling and belaying off one-, two-, and three-hundred foot cliffs. We spent days just learning the basics.

"John and Cindy," our climbing instructor said to us when he thought we were ready, "how'd you like to climb the Grand Teton mountain with me tomorrow?"

I looked at Cindy and then back at my guide. After several moments of weighing the misgivings I saw in Cindy's eyes against my own feelings and the confidence I sensed in the eyes of the instructor, I made a decision that launched me into a whole new realm of adventure and eventually took me all over the world.

"I think that would be an absolute thrill!" I said.

The next day we climbed all the way up to 11,500 feet, to the saddle between the Grand Teton peak and the other peaks. We camped overnight there so we'd be ready for the final assault at 3:00 the next morning.

At 2:00 A.M. we arose and began preparing for the long climb to the Grand Teton peak. But something was wrong. I looked over toward the Idaho side and saw a bank of clouds.

"We'd better wait," our guide said. "Those storms can be vicious and quite unpredictable at this altitude."

The clouds got closer and closer, and soon I felt little drops of rain beginning to fall on my face. The rain turned into sleet, hail, and then snow. Winds began to gust up to sixty and seventy miles an hour. Before long the cloud bank enveloped the mountain and the wind began to slap us. Within forty-five minutes there was seven inches of snow on the mountains, and with all that wind the snow was blowing into huge drifts.

"We've got to abort the climb," our guide shouted. "We've got to get down off this mountain!"

So down we came, holding onto rocks all the way to keep from being blown off. We couldn't wear our glasses because the gusting and driving snow would white them out in a few seconds. You can't imagine how tough it was to climb down the slippery rocks and stumble over the boulders and cliffs without our glasses, which we always wear.

For me the Grand Teton was my first great mountain-climbing experience; Cindy proclaimed it was her last. I had developed confidence and technical skills, and I knew that I could mountain climb. I knew I could be hanging out over a thousand-foot precipice and still be able to function. However, it had become painfully obvious to me, as I remembered the suffering I'd experienced during that aborted climb, how big a role physical fitness plays in high-altitude mountain climbing. Other sports, like tennis, golf, and racquetball, can be enjoyed on a more recreational basis, though the better shape you're in, the better you'll play. But mountain climbing involves a tremendous amount of energy, requires continual exertion, and makes severe demands on the legs, lungs, and heart. The thinning air at high altitudes makes the lungs and heart work much harder just to keep up with the normal climbing activities.

Stamina—that's what it takes! It's not optional—your life depends on it. But how could a guy who lives in the flatlands of Indiana build the kind of stamina that would hold up under such demands? There was only one way I could think of, but for several months I refused to acknowledge it. The only activity that could train my body and mind to develop the necessary stamina was a full-scale marathon. That grueling, 26.2-mile classic challenge was just what I needed. If I could train my thirty-four-year-old body and get it in shape to run a complete marathon, I knew I would have the confidence to build up my stamina for a major climb.

During the next four months I doubled and then tripled my mileage, taking it up to forty and fifty miles a week. On the last seven weekends before I was scheduled to run the marathon I took runs of fifteen and twenty miles. Between working, running, and recuperating, I didn't do much else.

Then on June 2, 1979, my family and I headed for Terre Haute, Indiana, where they hold one of the top ten marathons in the country. I don't remember much about the marathon except that at 7:00 in the morning the gun went off and I headed out on those Indiana country roads, running at my predetermined pace.

By the time I reached the twenty-one mile water station, my vision was blurred by sweat. All I could see in front of me was a little brown-haired head on the left, and soon a little blond head on the right. As I got a little closer I realized that it was my four-year-old son, Ken, and my six-year-old daughter, Elise. It was all I could do to manage a smile. Ken held out a sponge. I took it and wiped my brow with it. When I came to Elise, she handed me a cup of water. I drank about half of it and poured the rest down the back of my neck. As I picked up my pace coming out of that water station, I heard from behind me the most glorious and inspirational little voice. It was Elise yelling at the top of her lungs, "Come on, Daddy, come on, Daddy, you can do it! You've only got five more miles to go!"

Do you think there was any way I wasn't going to make it after encouragement like that? I looked down at my feet, as I'd done so often on long runs, and they were going back and forth, back and forth. But they felt heavier and heavier, like two soggy logs.

I passed the twenty-two-mile mark, the twenty-three-mile mark, the twenty-four- and twenty-five-mile marks. Confidence began to build within me. I knew I was going to make it. In fact, I knew I could walk the last few miles and still make it; but the marathon (just like life) is not designed to be walked. It's designed to be run—every step of the way.

At last, I could see it—the Terre Haute County Fair and the huge banner stretched across the road: FINISH LINE—MARATHON. It had taken all I had, but I finished that marathon on the run, and what a thrill it was. If I live to be a thousand years old, I'll never forget the joy of hearing my two children at the finish line shouting, "Daddy, you made it!"

At Last—I Was Here

As the temperature dropped lower and lower that night in the rugged little cabin, I pulled the three army blankets up tighter around my chin to seal in as much body heat as I could. I thought about that picture of the Matterhorn hanging in my den, how I'd looked longingly at it the day I'd hung it there, and how I'd followed one intermediate goal after another to this almost mystical moment in my life. The Matterhorn had seemed so far away when I'd started. At last I was here; tomorrow was to be the day!

Just before I dozed off to sleep, I looked up at the ceiling and asked the Lord to take control and become my "Guide of guides," to help me make it safely to the top and back down. I prayed that it might be His will for me to share this experience for His glory, and for the benefit of others.

I closed the prayer by asking Him to help me keep my Five High Climbing Do's and Don'ts focused clearly in my mind during the entire climb tomorrow:

1. Do everything my guide tells me, every step of the way.
2. Place my hands and feet exactly where he places his above me.
3. Don't give up—no matter how much it starts to hurt.
4. Never ask the psychologically defeating question, how much farther is it?
5. Remember all the way up that the most difficult part of the climb is the climb down.

Having prayed, I knew I needed to sleep, and sleep I did.

The Long-Awaited Climb

At exactly 3:00 A.M. there was a knock on the door from Alfons. I'd slept in my climbing clothes, so all I had to do was put on my boots and fold the blankets, and I was ready to go downstairs for a light breakfast.

As we left the cabin, we were greeted by four other climbing parties, all experienced European climbers. They leered at me, as if to say, who does this silly American think he is, taking on the Matterhorn with only two years' experience climbing mountains? I have to admit their attitude bothered me, but I knew I couldn't let it intimidate me. I had to concentrate entirely on what I was doing and trust Alfons's every move. After all, Alfons had told me, "We could make it *together*."

We began our climb up the narrow northeast ridge. Rock by rock we climbed. Alfons took the lead, and I just tried to stay close enough to keep the rope slack between us. An almost-full moon lit up the boulder field with an eerie glow. The stars at ten thousand feet in the Swiss Alps are absolutely fantastic. Every square inch of the sky is covered in heavenly hues of green, pale blue, and orange.

Soon we reached the base of the cliffs and started climbing them. At first they were not too steep, but that soon changed. Our climbing method was the classic Alpine style of 30- to 150-foot pitches. Alfons would climb on ahead and anchor the rope, pull it taut between us, and yell down "Climb!" I'd reply, "Climbing," and up I'd go, making sure that at least three of my limbs were always fixed firmly on the rock holds, while the fourth pressed upward for a higher hold. The taut belay rope would assure my safety, so that if I fell, I'd only fall a foot or so. For two solid hours we climbed without a break. The pace began to tell on me. I could sense that the cold, the thin air of the high altitude, and the strong winds were beginning to take their toll.

Shortly before 6:00 A.M., the glow of the dawn began to appear like a knife's edge on the horizon, and I could see that the sharp drop to the glacier floor below had grown considerably during the two hours we'd been climbing. But I wasn't afraid because I had complete trust in my guide, and because I was concentrating so intensely that there was no time to think about possible danger.

The First Great Challenge

We came to the Shoulder, the first of two great challenges facing the Matterhorn climber. This massive bulge, 1,300 stories above sea level, loomed like a gigantic obstacle that stood between us and our goal. A two-inch diameter hemp rope was attached to the side of the shoulder. It was covered with ice and snow. We put on our leather gloves and started climbing up that slippery rope. Again, Alfons went first, climbing to the top of a ledge, securing the belay rope, and calling down for me to follow. Hand over hand I crept upward, always making sure to keep both my feet on the mountain. Pitch after pitch, for what seemed like hours, we climbed. Climbing that shoulder at sea level would be hard enough, but at 13,000 feet it was devastating.

Suddenly, I noticed that my hands were getting numb. The tips of my fingers began to sting and then burn. Was this frostbite? Off came my gloves. I blew feverishly into my cupped hands again and again, trying to restore the feeling and control.

"Climb!" came the command from above. But I was still blowing into my hands.

"What are you doing down there, John?" Alfons demanded.

"I'm blowing on my hands, Alfons!" I shouted back.

"We don't have time for that. Climb!" he barked like a drill sergeant.

"But Alfons, my hands—they're freezing!" I pleaded.

"Beat 'em on the rocks!" he commanded. Was he serious? Beat them on the rocks? But, I remembered, "Do everything my guide tells me every step of the way." So, slap! Slap! Slap! Within a minute, I'd beaten the feeling back into my hands.

"Now continue to beat your hands on the rocks the rest of the way up. Do you understand me?" he yelled.

"Yes, sir," I said humbly. And I kept beating my hands on the rocks at each pitch.

The Greatest Challenge

Just as I was nearing exhaustion, we came to the most difficult obstacle on the Matterhorn—the notorious Overhang. It's a five-story cliff that juts out into space, exposing the climber to a mile-long drop straight to the glacier floor. Again, there was a two-inch diameter hemp rope hanging over the upper edge of the Overhang. It was twisting and swirling furiously in the wind that blew constantly at this high altitude. Alfons threw out a lariat, lassoed the rope, and pulled it in. Without the slightest hesitation, he grabbed the rope and started up.

I welcomed this short breather while Alfons climbed. While I was resting, I had time to think about how dangerous this Overhang really was. It had been the scene of the most horrible mountaineering accident ever. In 1865, on the first successful conquest of the Matterhorn, the Sir Edward Whymper party had reached the top and half of them had started back down. There were four climbers on one rope. The first climber on the rope was inexperienced—he slipped and plummeted off the top edge of the Overhang. The other three climbers, joined together on that same rope, tumbled and plunged the long mile through space to their deaths on the glacier floor below.

When the command came from above me to climb, I grabbed hold of the rope and started upward. I tried not to think about that accident and concentrated totally on what I was doing. Keeping my feet anchored firmly on the rocks was absolutely essential, because swinging out from the mountain on the rope would have been too strenuous for my arms. Higher and higher I climbed, up and up, hand over hand, one foot then the other. As I struggled over the ledge at the top of the Overhang, I was gasping for more oxygen to fill my burning lungs and replenish my fatigued cardiovascular system.

As Alfons and I sat down on a rock, I could tell his supreme confidence in my conditioning was on the wane. We paused for about three minutes to strap on our steel crampons, or spikes, for the last thousand feet of the climb up a snow-banked incline. Now we would have to climb with our heels instead of our toes. Step by step, I gasped for the ever-thinning air. The pain was constant, the exhaustion almost complete, but the widening blue sky above, beside, and below me kept pushing me onward and upward.

The Summit

13,800 feet, 14,000, 14,200 feet, 14,400, 14,700 feet. Suddenly I bumped right into the back of Alfons and almost knocked him off the mountain!

"Oh my goodness," I thought, "I'm in for the worst tongue-lashing any mountain climber ever received!" Instead, he turned, and in a calm voice said, "Easy John, but come up here beside me." I worked my way up the narrow ice ridge and stood tenuously beside him, bent over, still gasping for air. Alfons put his arm around me and said, "Get your eyes up. This is your dream. You are—*on top of the Matterhorn!*"

What a sight—all sky! But I must report accurately that there was no great feeling of joy, no great ecstasy, nor any of the other emotions the mountaineering books promise you'll have when you reach the summit of a great mountain. I was gasping for breath. My lungs were burning. My legs shook with fatigue and muscle spasms. Only one word could describe what I felt in my moment of victory: *meekness*.

But what a suprise the Matterhorn holds for those who reach its peak. It's not a peak at all! There, 14,780 feet in the air, is what looks like a football field—one hundred yards long, but only twenty-eight inches wide, like a crescent in the sky.

Two minutes after Alfons had spoken we were sitting astraddle the top of that ridge, with one leg in Italy and the other in Switzerland. Alfons pulled out a little piece of German chocolate, a wedge of cheese, and some kind of clear liquid, and we proceeded to have the most spectacular picnic I'd ever attended. The Belgian climber who had snickered at me previously came up to the top, and we exchanged "summit shot" pictures. The last picture I took on top of the Matterhorn, however, was a picture I'd seen many times in my mind, a picture of my feet standing on its peak. I wanted to have that picture as a remembrance that my feet had actually stood on top of the Matterhorn.

The Climb Down

The summit ritual lasted only twenty minutes, and then Alfons turned around and was all business again.

"John Noe," he said with the sternest look I'd yet seen him give, "I'm going to be very, very angry with you if you don't do everything I tell you to do on the way down."

"Yes, sir," I again replied meekly.

"You must go first," he ordered.

As I started down, I reminded myself of my fifth rule, "Remember that the most difficult part of the climb is the climb down." It was on the descent that most of the major accidents among mountain climbers had occurred. It was on the way down that concentration tended to become lax and climbers would make foolish, even fatal, errors. The descent required continual technical correctness and was mentally exhausting.

Alfons barked out a continuous series of instructions from above. "Right! Left! Down! Feel that toe hold?"

"No, where?" I cried.

"Six inches to the right, feel it?" he continued.

Each time that I blindly searched for an elusive toe hold, I reminded myself of what he had told me before we began our slow and laborious descent: I had to go first so he could hold the rope and secure me from above.

"John," he'd told me, "sometimes you're going to have to face outward and reach down with your hands. At other times you'll turn your face into the mountain and feel blindly below for the toeholds. But you're not to worry," he reassured, "I have you on the rope—and I am the *best*!"

By now, I'd developed complete trust in this man who held my life on the end of a rope. So down I went, trying my best to do everything he told me exactly as he told me to do it. It was four hours of the most intense and exhausting work I've ever done in my life. We came down over the Overhang, the Shoulder, the cliffs, through the traverses, and down the northeast ridge. When we reached the boulder fields, I could relax my concentration slightly, and I started to remember all the fears and doubts that had plagued me for the past two years as I'd prepared myself for this climb.

"Could I make it?" I'd wondered. "Should I even attempt it?" How insignificant my fears seemed now. I remembered the surges of momentum I'd always felt after I'd reached each intermediate goal. I thought about how much farther I could see and how much clearer the visions of the future had seemed after I'd reached an intermediate goal. Now I wondered if the climb to the top of the Matterhorn might someday turn into an intermediate goal for something else.

At that moment, a huge mental avalanche assaulted me. I turned around and looked up at that mighty obelisk we were still descending, and I was forced into a deep confession.

"John," I said to myself, "there is no way that you could have ever climbed a mountain as magnificent as the Matterhorn without the expert guidance of Alfons Franzen." I also realized that there was no way I could have qualified for the climb up the Matterhorn had it not been for the guidance of the instructors at the mountain-climbing school the summer before. Without the books and teachers guiding me I'd never have made it. Most of all, I knew that God, my "Guide of guides," had made it possible for me to accomplish this great feat. The greatest delusion in the world is that of the so-called "self-made" person. There is no such thing in high achievement.

What About Your Dream?

Do you have a dream? Do you have a burning desire to accomplish something great in your life? If you want to reach out and touch the sky, if you want to reach your full potential as a human being, created in the image of God, read on.

In this book, I'm going to share with you the magnificent secrets I've learned from all the expert guides who've helped me become successful, not only as a mountain climber, but as a family man, a businessman, a Christian, a speaker, and a human being.

2

Achievers vs. High Achievers

As I reflect on how much I endured during the two-year "climb" to the top of the Matterhorn, as well as the effort it took to reach that high goal, I can understand why most people are content to float through life, taking whatever comes easily.

There are basically three categories of people in our society:

1. The *nonachievers*—passive people who stand around waiting for something to happen. You'll find them in subordinate jobs for ten, twenty, or even thirty years. Nonachievers are satisfied to let others set goals for them. They like the comfort of being told what to do at every turn and the security of stable conditions. Oh, they might grumble about the decisions others make for them and secretly wish for independence. They might even dream that someday they'll break out and achieve distinction. But nonachievers never seem to leave the crowd because they are content to have shallow goals set for them and to do no more than what's expected.

2. The *achievers*—those who want to make things happen. You'll find them setting their own goals, venturing out into untested waters, and performing "above and beyond the call of duty." Many of the achievers will set goals that require a great deal of effort and persistence to reach. They are basically self-motivated, self-directed, and self-determined. You'll never find them depending on society, because they cherish their independence. Among the achievers you'll find many successful salespeople, lawyers, doctors, business leaders, and community leaders. They are usually respected, admired, and well-liked.

3. But then there are the *high achievers*—the people who will not settle for one bit less than their full potential as human beings. They might fall into the same careers as the achievers, but you'll find the high achievers pushing themselves beyond normal human endurance, setting goals that are considered unreachable by most people, and imaginatively choosing the things they want to make happen. High achievers are constantly stretching their minds, wills, and bodies to surpass their limitations. They won't always be successful. In fact, sometimes you'll find them failing time and time again because their reach may exceed their grasp. But often enough they'll reach their incredible goals—goals so high they'll shock even the achievers.

Don't expect everybody to like or understand high achievers. It takes a special kind of mentality to become a high achiever. The average person simply cannot grasp what it is that drives the high achiever to perform at such exhausting levels.

Nonachievers are satisfied to be happy, or content, or maybe even apathetic and complacent. They're always looking for what they call "the good life," and they live by the hedonistic philosophy: If it feels good, do it!

The achievers, on the other hand, tend to be activists who get involved and work toward becoming successful. Very often they define success in material terms through status symbols and recognition for their accomplishments. They're willing to put aside the fun-for-the-moment attitude in order to build better lives for themselves. Usually they set and live by goals that are important to them. Their motto is: What the mind can conceive and believe, it can achieve.

But the high achievers are driven by forces beyond themselves. They've caught a glimpse of the best life, and will not settle for anything less. You'll find them constantly pushing against their own limits, deeply and personally involved in whatever they're doing, sometimes practically torturing themselves to achieve their high goals.

Who is it that we admire most as a high achiever? It's the poor kid who amasses a fortune, the blind person who climbs to the top of Mount Rainier, the paralyzed victim who comes back and runs the marathon, the disabled veteran who becomes a Super Bowl champion, or the child with a speech impediment who becomes a great speaker. Do we admire them because they are handicapped, or disadvantaged, or lacking resources? No. We admire them because they set high goals and become high achievers.

I have no intention of telling you where you fit in my breakdown of the nonachievers, achievers, and high achievers. Only you can make that selection. All I've tried to do is to give you some guidelines to help you discover the pattern you've lived by up to now. Furthermore, it is not my intention to tell you that you should reach for a higher category. That choice is always yours. But I suspect that those who are still reading would fall into the category of achievers who have some desire to go on to become high achievers. Most of the non-achievers probably put this book down early in the first chapter and turned on their television sets. They wanted simply to be entertained.

If you are an achiever and have a strong desire to become a high achiever, I believe I can help you do it. You see, I've been there. I've had the opportunity to learn from the best.

What is a High Achiever?

The best way to define high achievement is in terms of the type of goal set and then reached. Most people are satisfied with goals as they are defined by the dictionary. According to *Webster's New Collegiate Dictionary*, a goal is "the end toward which effort is directed." This definition states that a goal is anything toward which a person works. Everybody sets goals. Even the nonachiever sets goals. It may be nothing more than the goal of still being among the living at quitting time, but even that's a goal.

Achievers set goals that require effort and determination to reach. They want to increase their sales by 10 percent, or step up their production by some measured amount, or get something they desire. And don't misunderstand me, these are good goals; they'll take you far in life. But high achievement comes only from setting and attaining what I call *high goals!* A goal is a target you can *reach alone*. However, a high goal is a goal that is so far beyond your grasp you *must have help in reaching it*. A high goal is one that you can only attain with the help of others.

Now in my own life, I go one step farther in setting my goals. I set what I call *God-sized goals*. A God-sized goal is one that is so far beyond your human capabilities that you will never reach it unless God intervenes on your behalf.

Climbing the Matterhorn was more than a high goal for me, it was a God-sized goal. Sure, I had to do everything I could to prepare myself for that gigantic climb. I had to push myself beyond all of my former limits, following Alfons every step of the way, doing everything exactly as he told me to do it. That was my part. Yet, when I had reached the end of my conditioned strength and exhausted the stamina I had developed, I felt a surge of God's strength and power pulling me along. Without those boosts from Him I'd never have made it.

High Goals Must Be Personal and Timely

High achievement for one person may not be high achievement for another. What is a high goal for me may not be a high goal for you. Not everybody wants to climb the Matterhorn, and I don't think that everybody should try to climb that awesome mountain. And climbing the Matterhorn was not a high goal for Alfons: It was part of his daily life.

High goals must be very personal. They must be set high enough to stretch your imagination, your boundaries, and your capabilities more than ever before.

High goals must also be timely. A high goal today may not be a high goal tomorrow. What causes me to reach out for help at one stage of my life may not be worthy of my efforts at a later stage.

I'm sure there was a time when climbing to the top of

the Matterhorn was a very high goal for Alfons
Franzen. Surely the first time he climbed to the little
cabin at 10,500 feet, over the Shoulder and Overhang,
up to the peak of the world's most famous mountain, it
was a high achievement for even that great mountaineer.

Maybe you were a high achiever yesterday, or when
you were in college, or in high school. Perhaps you've
reached the peak of some high goal you once set for
yourself, and you have since become complacent. But
yesterday's high goals only become useful to us when we
use them as launching pads from which to reach even
higher goals.

The Great Myth of Self-Motivation

For most of the last two decades we've been bombarded
with books, tapes, and speeches on self-motivation.
Some of us have become tired from hearing about it at
every turn. My promise is that this is not going to be
another book on self-motivation. This promise is an
easy one to keep since I outright reject the basic idea of
self-motivation.

You've heard the pitches, I'm sure: Think positively!
Believe you can do it, and you can do it! Take charge of
your own life! Pull yourself up by your own bootstraps!
Get yourself going . . . .

Many of us have benefited from self-motivation
theories because they work—up to a point. A person
who is always pessimistic or lazy or has an inferiority
complex can improve his or her performance tremen-
dously through self-motivation. However, self-motivation theories eventually begin to cave in under their own

weight because there is only so far they can go. People begin to say, Oh, no. Not another self-motivation speaker—we had one of those last year! Management circles, I've found, are tired of the hype, the rah-rah pep talks, the glorified weather reports, and the positive thinking. For many of them, self-motivation has led to frustration. It's superficial and limited in its effectiveness.

I believe that self-motivation is a false concept of human behavior and that it goes against the Word of God because it is based on three fallacies:

1. Self-motivation theories usually divide man into only two dimensions—the body and the mind. The idea is that if the mind controls the body, the body can be made to do anything the mind can dream of doing. Man is treated purely as a mind-body interaction. Man's third dimension, his spiritual dimension, is totally avoided.

2. Self-motivation is based on a misconception of the nature of man. The idea is, You've got a lot of goodness in you, and all you've got to do is let it out! Of course this thought is very attractive. It implies that every person is naturally good inside and has everything necessary to build an ideal life.

Self-motivators are obsessed with self-expression, self-satisfaction, self-image, self-actualization, and self-sufficiency. This obsession with the self has led to the "me generation." But many of us consider that man is not good by nature, that we have evil within us. The self-motivated generation seems to have produced a greater proportion of self-centered and anxiety-plagued people in our country than at any other time in history. The root of many of our social problems, our disharmony, and our distress is self-centeredness, the very building block on which self-motivation rests.

3. Self-motivation is based on deception. It is built on the idea that one can deceive oneself into becoming successful, better, and happier.

Self-motivators use "self-talk" to induce themselves to have a positive frame of mind. ("I feel healthy, I feel happy, I feel terrific.") They think that if they repeat the words often enough, they'll believe them and begin acting upon them, thus achieving the desired result. The idea of deceiving yourself into becoming successful by making yourself "feel" successful is limited. Eventually your mind begins to demand a stronger form of motivation.

That brings us to the only motivating force that has the potential to make you become all that you were created to be—a high achiever.

Out-of-Self Motivation

First, *out-of-self motivation* goes beyond self-motivation. It recognizes that human beings are three-dimensional. We have a mind, a body, and a spirit. Our spiritual dimension deserves at least as much attention as do our mind and body. It needs to be fed and exercised or it gets weak and ineffective. We humans work as a system; our various parts are interdependent. We are complete beings: mental, physical, and spiritual.

Secondly, out-of-self motivation asserts that man is not necessarily good by nature. We are standing in the way of our own success. We are our own greatest hurdle.

Shakespeare said it in *Julius Caesar*:

> The fault, dear Brutus, is not in the stars,
> But in ourselves.

Sir Edmund Hillary, the New Zealander who first set foot on the top of the world's highest mountain, Mount Everest, said, "It's not the mountain we conquer, but ourselves." Even Albert Einstein knew it: "The real problem is in the hearts and minds of men. It is not a problem of physics but of ethics. It is easier to denature plutonium than to denature the evil spirt of man."

Out-of-self motivation faces with candor what we are really like inside. Each of us has an imperfection, a built-in limitation: the "self." It must be dealt with and overcome before motivation can become effective for reaching our high goals.

The basic building block of out-of-self motivation is that there is only one person in the universe who is worthy, who has enough to offer, to become the center of our lives—Jesus Christ, God's son. The goal is, then, to become Christ-directed rather than self-directed. Out-of-self motivation is based on the biblical principle of receiving a "higher self" by surrendering our old selfish nature to Jesus Christ. Then and only then can we receive God's wisdom and power in our lives.

This fact is important in becoming a high achiever because people will do things for God that they will not do for themselves.

Thirdly, out-of-self motivation is not based on deception, but on truth. It holds that God can be with us and wants us to set high goals. He will help us become high achievers if we will follow His lead in our thoughts and actions.

The most powerful motivation available to people today is the reality that God loves them and is inside them,
and that all His resources are available to them as they
pursue goals as high achievers.

Stretching Ourselves
Toward Motivation

In 1973, I became a member of an international good-
will ambassador team. I spent three months in India,
Nepal, and Bangladesh living with families, speaking
with people, visiting schools and universities, and studying industries. This intimate, firsthand exposure to such
a magnificent kaleidoscope of people and places was a
mind-stretching experience for me.

When I came back to the United States, I realized that
I had been changed. I knew that it was going to be very
difficult for me ever again to settle for the common, the
ordinary, or the dull. I'd given up forever my seat as a
"spectator in the arena of life." I had seen that life had
much more to offer than I had originally thought. For
those people who reach for it, life is one great adventure
after another. For those who set high goals for themselves, and then pursue them with all their energy, life
offers possibilities beyond our wildest imaginings.

The Muddle of Mediocrity

H. L. Mencken, the long-time editor of the famous
American Mercury magazine, was at one time the

foremost authority on American usage of English. But while a few people recognized his genius, most of those around him considered him eccentric. An often-told anecdote from the early days of his newspaper career illustrates why his peers found him hard to understand.

One day at a particularly quiet moment in the normally noisy newsroom where he worked, the young Mencken shouted at the top of his lungs, "It's coming in the doors!" Needless to say, everyone stopped and looked in his direction.

"It's up to the bottom of the desks!" said Mencken as he rose to his feet. "It's up to the seats of our chairs!" he shouted as he jumped onto his chair.

"What are you talking about?" asked one of his incredulous colleagues.

"It's up to the tops of our desks!" shouted Mencken as he jumped to the top of his desk.

"What do you mean?" rang a chorus of shouts.

"Mediocrity!" came the caustic reply. "We're drowning in mediocrity!" he shouted over and over as he jumped from the desk and rushed out the door, never to return.

Call him eccentric, call him hypercritical, call him what you will, but H. L. Mencken was not willing to drown in what he saw as a "sea of mediocrity."

If Mencken were alive today, he might very well climb to the top of the world's tallest building screaming that his country has become one giant muddle of mediocrity. I would agree. What we have done in this country is foster a plague of mediocrity—huge numbers of people who are content to drift with the tide. They range from social welfare recipients to people locked into jobs solely for financial considerations, from school dropouts to TV recluses. Masses of people flit from one thing to another, from one emotional high or low to another, or, even worse, just take things as they come. Far too many people have given up the hope of really living and have settled simply to exist amid the "good life" of mediocrity.

We human beings are made to be high achievers. When we settle for less, we become bored and frustrated. After all, we were created in the image of God, and there is no higher achiever in the universe than He.

Jack London wrote as his credo:

I would rather be ashes than dust!
I would rather
    that my spark should burn out in a brilliant
    blaze
    than it should be stifled by dry rot.
I would rather be a superb meteor,
    every atom of me in magnificent glow,
    than a sleepy and permanent planet.
The proper function of man is to live, not exist.
I shall not waste my days in trying to prolong them.
I shall use my time.[1]

Who Wants To Be a Mountain Climber?

Not many people want to climb the Matterhorn—or any mountain for that matter. But you don't have to climb the world's mountains to become a high achiever. There are high goals of many kinds. In each of our lives, there are dreams that inspire us to the greatness for which we were created. A high goal may be as personal as losing weight, or it could be a goal for our business, our family

[1] From *A Pictorial Life of Jack London*, by Russ Kingman, by permission of the Crown Publishing Group.

life, or our spiritual growth. High achievers can be found in community service work, in schools, in churches, and in every arena of human activity.

My first high goal was to start my own business when I was thirty years old. That was a high goal for me because it meant that I had to leave a secure job in a large corporation and fight for economic survival for several years. The expenditure of energy in pursuit of that high goal was enormous. For two years, the business lost money, and there were times I felt just as exhausted from the long hours of work and mental fatigue as I have felt while struggling against the elements of nature on long mountain climbs.

What's the dream you've held in the back of your mind for more years than you can count? What giant mountain peak is luring you? Perhaps you've always wanted to stretch your horizons, to make real your vision of high achievement. Maybe you do have what it takes to become a high achiever.

3

Ten Questions that Can Change Your Life

You don't look like a mountain climber! is one of the most frequent comments I receive from people after they've heard me speak about my experiences as a high achiever. High achievers come in all different shapes, sizes, and colors. When you first meet a high achiever whom you've long admired at a distance, it is not unusual to be shocked by his or her appearance; high achievers look like everybody else. You'll find them in a variety of careers, social settings, and fields of endeavor. But excepting superficial physical traits, high achievers are usually pretty easy to spot because they have a special aura: They're the ones who are always seeking something great to do, to experience, and to become.

The following questions can help you decide if you have what it takes to become a high achiever. They are designed to be seriously considered and answered from the deepest regions of your heart.

1.   Do you really want to become a high achiever? A

fellow mountain climber once told me that the key to all self-discipline is desire. Since becoming a high achiever requires so much self-discipline and such a large personal investment, it is important to have desire. Here are some factors that often separate a typical person from the high achiever.

First, high achievers usually must spend a great deal of time alone. Some people cannot tolerate solitude. Perhaps you are one of those individuals who is constantly immersed in the noise of a radio, a television set, or a stereo system. Maybe you find the idea of silence threatening. Or perhaps you feel that you must always be surrounded by supportive friends and associates who are constantly "stroking" you and giving you the reassurance of herd warmth. When you are alone, you tend to be overpowered by loneliness.

Most really creative pursuits require solitude and silence. It is in such an environment that true genius can flourish. Even when high achievers must work in a noisy environment, a crowded office, a busy thoroughfare, they seek the solitude of their own thoughts by blocking out all the distractions around them.

A good index for your tolerance for being alone is the degree to which acceptance by your peers is important to you. The best indicators are things like: how attracted you are to fads in clothing or automobiles; how conscious you are of status symbols such as big desks, fancy offices, and impressive-sounding titles; and how easily you pick up slang or jargon just because it is popular with a certain crowd you want to be a part of.

Before you say you want to become a high achiever, weigh carefully the consequences of that choice, which include being alone, being your own person.

Secondly, high achievers are constantly finding themselves in new situations. The idea of moving to a new

city, taking on a new job, or launching out onto a totally uncharted course is, for many people, a terrifying
experience. If you like your life neatly arranged into
comfortable compartments with no surprises, then it's
questionable whether you really desire to be a high
achiever. Often, the high achiever must risk everything
and face uncertainty. Knowing that you will be sub-
jected constantly to new situations and environments,
do you still want to become a high achiever?

Thirdly, high achievers must risk rejection by their
peers. Fear of rejection is one of the most paralyzing
forces that can seize the human spirit. In his essay "Self-
Reliance," Ralph Waldo Emerson wrote "To be great,
is to be misunderstood." If you study the biographies of
high achievers, you will discover that most of these people were misunderstood, often by those closest to them
who were unable to believe in their great future. If you
set your course toward becoming a high achiever, don't
expect even your closest relatives and associates to
understand you. The most you can realistically hope for
is that they will continue to love you.

Before you decide you want to become a high
achiever, weigh the adversity of living without feeling
supported and approved of.

2. Do you have a strong inner urge to reach out?
The urge to create, to achieve, to reach for new experiences is like a compressed spring inside the high
achiever. Truman Capote, one of the most famous writers of our generation, was once asked by the editor of
Mademoiselle magazine, "Why do you write?" He responded by saying, "The serious artist, like Proust, is
like an object caught by a huge wave and swept to shore.
He's obsessed by his material; it's like a venom working
in his blood and the art is the antidote."

If you have this kind of creative urge, you have one of

the necessary ingredients for becoming a high achiever.

3.   *What matters most to you?* The key question for the high achiever is never What have you done? but What have you become? The real measure of a person is what that person values. What do you value most? Is it money? Recognition? Material possessions?

In the famous French story *The Little Prince*, the dearest friend the main character makes on the fictitious planet to which he has been banished is a fox. When the fox must leave the little prince forever, he offers to tell him the most wonderful secret in the world if the prince meets certain conditions. When he's met all the conditions, the little prince asks to be told the greatest secret. "Only that which is invisible is essential," the fox replies.

How much value do you place upon the intangible qualities of life that are so essential to becoming a high achiever? Some of these qualities are self-respect, pride of accomplishment, the capacity for love, and a positive outlook.

The path is often rough for the high achiever, and during those tough times you need more than material motivations to keep you moving.

4.   *What are you willing to invest?* High achievment requires an enormous amount of energy, time, effort, and commitment. As I said in the first chapter, one of the most self-defeating questions you can ever ask on a long mountain climb is, How long will it take? But, you ask, don't I have a right to ask how much of an investment will be required to become a high achiever? The answer to that question is a little like the one given by the financier who was asked by a young executive who had seen the business tycoon's huge yacht, "How much does it cost to buy a yacht like that?"

"Young man," replied the financier, "if you have to ask, you can't afford it!"

Michelangelo, whose sculpture and paintings have been famous for more than four centuries, did not become a great painter and sculptor overnight. Although he had great talents and genius, his accomplishments came only after he had invested himself to the point of physical exhaustion in becoming one of the greatest artists who ever lived. He spent years lying flat on his back on a scaffold to paint the fresco in the Sistine Chapel. By the time he had finished, he was virtually blind from the paint that had dripped into his eyes. He spent the remainder of his life in near blindness. Now, that's a real investment!

In answering the main question of this chapter, Do you have what it takes to become a high achiever?, you must answer the question, What are you willing to invest? The answer should be that you are willing to invest whatever it takes.

5. *How much are you willing to endure?* "Life does not ask simply how much can you do? It asks, also, how much can you endure, and still be unspoiled?" wrote Harry Emerson Fosdick in *The Manhood of the Master.* In the same work he exclaimed, "What a testing of character adversity is!"

The problems of life have a way of cascading down upon the individual who sets his course to become a high achiever. Relentlessly, adversities dog his every step. Those who have what it takes to become high achievers learn to endure whatever difficulties they encounter, and they transform difficulties into opportunities.

There is no room in the life of the high achiever for pettiness. It is destructive to complain about how you have been treated or what obstacles you have encountered. When the going gets tough, it is the weak who complain—the high achiever shifts gears, and keeps going.

How much are you willing to endure? To that question, those who have what it takes to become high achievers answer, Whatever I must endure!

6.   *What are you willing to give up?* While in San Francisco recently, I had the opportunity to take the "grand prix" course at Bob Bondurant's school of high-performance driving. In high-performance driving there are four tire patches, and they are the only contact areas you have with the road. To become a high-performance driver, you must be sensitive to the signals that are picked up by the tires and transferred to the wheels, suspension, car seat, and controls. The first thing you notice about a high-performance race car is that it looks and feels different from the typical sedan made in Detroit. Regular car manufacturers build their modern cars with the intent of isolating the driver from the bumping of the tires on the road. The goal is to make the car comfortable, not to create an environment for high-performance driving.

Society today does the same thing to us. It desensitizes and isolates us from the bumps that are necessary for high-performance living. Most people are satisfied to seek "comfort levels," rather than go for high performance.

Everything around us is geared for comfortable living rather than high achievement. Once you decide to become a high achiever, you discover very quickly that you must constantly be willing to give up momentary pleasures and reach for your long-term goals. Remember this: Whatever you give yourself to, it always becomes your master.

7. How much responsibility are you willing to assume? There are millions of people who can do a job that is thrust upon them and enforced by close supervision. There is a great need in every area of human endeavor today for people who will assume responsibility. You won't find high achievers complaining about demanding jobs, little vacation time, or low benefits and salaries. You'll find them focusing their attention on how they can do a better job for their employer, or even how they can start their own business and take on all of the responsibilities that entails.

High achievement and responsibility go hand in hand. You cannot have one without the other.

8. Are you willing to start where you are? It is one thing to dream high and lofty dreams but quite another to make those dreams come true. "A journey of a thousand miles begins with a single step," says the wise old Oriental proverb.

Think about it! We spend approximately 6 percent of our income on food, approximately 12 percent on maintaining our automobiles; yet how many of us are spending 5 percent of our annual income on personal growth? How many of us are investing eight hours each week developing our personal potential? Our dreams for high achievement can only become reality when we are willing to take the first small step toward fulfilling them. Too many of us are satisfied to be like the old farmer who was once asked for directions to a nearby city. "Mister," he replied, "you can't get there from here."

Remember this: You can always get to where you want to go, providing you are willing to start from where you are. Start doing what you can do, and then reach out for those things you cannot do now. For example, if you want to become a great artist and all you can draw are stick figures, draw the best stick figures you can while studying the higher techniques from skilled artists and teachers. If you can't be perfect, be the best you can.

9. *Are you willing to think for yourself?* Someone once asked Joseph D. Kennedy, father of President John F. Kennedy, when it was that he started to make large amounts of money. He replied, "When I stopped pushing for it and went up and sat on the Cape and gave myself time to think."

One of the great myths that keep people from becoming high achievers is the idea that the harder you work, the more you will accomplish. It is true that there is no substitute for honest, hard work. However, it is equally important to achieve a balance between thought and action.

If you are willing to think for yourself rather than have someone else always do your thinking for you, you have what it takes to become a high achiever.

10. *Are you willing to settle for nothing less than your full potential?* Many people who have been high achievers are now failures because they refused to keep reaching out to become more than they were. They have become what I call *sustainers*.

"Success has ruined many a man," wrote Benjamin Franklin in *Poor Richard*. The person who reaches a modicum of success at an early age and spends the remainder of his or her life defending what has been gained must be considered a failure. High achievers continue to set very high goals for themselves—goals that are so high they can only be reached with the help of others.

If you are to become a high achiever, you must be willing to settle for nothing less than reaching your full potential as a human being created in the image and likeness of God.

You Can Too!

I believe that you have what it takes to become a high achiever. I believe that the potential for reaching high goals was placed within each of us by the Creator. Maybe you have not become sensitive to that potential. Or maybe you don't know how to develop it. But the ability lies within you because you are a human being.

I have experienced the exhilaration of high achievements, even God-sized achievements, and I believe you can too. You too can climb great mountains. You too can stand on top of the world. You too can feel the joy of high achievement, if you're willing. Are you willing?

PART TWO

Six Attitudes of High Achievers

The previous chapter outlined what it takes to be a high achiever. If you have the raw material, then read on! Here are six basic attitudes that you must adopt if you want to develop your raw material and realize your ultimate potential. Each of these attitudes is essential to becoming a high achiever, yet each one can be cultivated by any individual.

1. High achievers make no small plans.
2. High achievers are willing to do what they fear.
3. High achievers are willing to prepare.
4. High achievers are willing to risk failure.
5. High achievers are teachable.
6. High achievers have heart.

As you read about each attitude, ask yourself if this is the way you normally think about life, and if not, if this is the kind of outlook you would like to have.

4

High Achievers Make No Small Plans

Early in my corporate career, I had the privilege of sitting at the feet of a man who told me a personal story about himself and President Harry S. Truman. The story had such a powerful impact on me that it still affects everything I do.

The man, Wilson Wyatt, Sr., past mayor of Louisville, Kentucky, and a highly respected leader in the National Democratic Party, had always been recognized as a "guy who could get things done." In 1945, President Truman asked him to accept the position of National Housing Expediter and Administrator of the National Housing Agency. His job would be to develop and execute the post-war housing program. For many years there had been a shortage of residential buildings in the United States. This shortage had become more acute during the four years of World War II, when only 250,000 housing units had been constructed each year. With this shortage and the demobilization of several million American soldiers (most of whom wanted to start a home of their own almost immediately), President Truman regarded the housing program as one of this country's most pressing concerns. In appointing Wyatt, the president enjoined him that he should "make no small plans."

After carefully reviewing the situation and meeting with various influential groups nationwide, Wyatt announced a program to start 1.2 million residential buildings during 1946. That was approximately five times the number of houses built during the previous year.

Many national housing experts attacked the plan as an impossible goal. They reasoned that to move from a standstill in new housing in 1945 to the highest number of housing units ever begun in the world in one year would be totally beyond the grasp of the construction industry—particularly with all the material shortages in the immediate post-war era. However, from the very beginning, Wyatt took those four words from the president seriously. Throughout that year, whenever he or his staff would encounter almost insurmountable obstacles, they would remind themselves that the president had requested they "make no small plans."

The results were extraordinary. By the end of 1946, more than one million units had been started. While the achievement fell short of the goal, it was generally agreed that a significant factor in achieving so much was the high goal established from the beginning.

That story has served as a source of inspiration for me and many of my friends. All high achievers have this basic attitude, and they manifest it in everything they do.

That four-word phrase, "make no small plans," seized my imagination after I had heard Wyatt's story. Three years later I had those words engraved on a large plaque which now hangs on the wall in my office. It serves as a constant reminder to me whenever I need to make a decision. But, be forewarned! You never know how those words are going to change even the little things in your life. The decisions that continuously shape our lives are the little decisions. Each day we make hundreds of little choices that affect the big decisions of our lives.

Making no small plans starts with getting control of little choices such as: "How are you going to spend this day? What do you do when you're bored? What do you do that you don't have to do? What do you do when you don't have to do anything? What do you do first, second, and third, today?

Little Decisions Often Have Lasting Impact

During a trip with my family to Washington, D.C., over a Halloween weekend, I was presented with an excellent opportunity to put my "make no small plans" credo to the test. Our children, then six and eight years old, were enjoying seeing all the monuments, space exhibits, the White House, Capitol Hill, and other historic sites. Yet they were disappointed to be away from their friends, and they missed the trick-or-treating around our neighborhood.

As we sat eating dinner at the hotel on Halloween night, both children were quite somber.

"We could go trick-or-treat at the White House," I kidded.

"We couldn't do that!" exclaimed my daughter. "Whoever heard of trick-or-treating at the White House?"

"I guess you're right," I responded, figuring that would end the conversation.

"But, Daddy," my son exclaimed, "don't you believe in making no small plans?"

What could I say? After my son had challenged me with my own credo, there was nothing left to do but set about to trick-or-treat at the White House. So off we went, up to our hotel room to put together some sort of costume for our two kids to wear.

Soon we were standing in front of the White House. Two little kids, somewhat more scared than scary-looking, timidly approached the spotlighted and glass-enclosed guardhouse on the White House grounds.

As the children drew closer, an authoritative voice demanded through the speaker system, "What do you want?"

"Trick-or-treat," two quaky, pleading little voices replied to the invisible interrogator.

"Come through the gate and up to the window," the voice ordered.

As my two children gingerly approached the mirror-like window, a mechanical teller drawer slowly extended out from the wall and opened up. Inside the drawer was a bag of jelly beans. My kids were thrilled! They had trick-or-treated at the White House—all because one of them had reminded me of the importance of making no small plans in even the smallest choices of life.

We make many little choices that either lead us ever upward or lead us along the path of mediocrity. The difference between the two is whether we "make no small plans"—not just in the few big decisions of our lives, but in all the little choices.

Making No Small Plans Attracts Big People

There is something contagious about making no small plans and setting high goals. Great plans and high goals attract big people. They attract power, energy, and commitment. Simple goals and small plans attract small people, low power, weak energy, and lack of commitment. You will never get anywhere in life with small thinking.

Think of the response NASA would have received as it tried to recruit astronauts for the moon shot, if it had made small plans. "Gentlemen," a NASA leader might have said, "we are going to attempt to get a man off the ground and see how far we can shoot him into the air. We might eventually even try to break out of the earth's atmosphere, and see how far we can go into space." If you had been in a room filled with budding young astronauts, you would probably have seen a mass evacuation. With small plans like that there would have been no way NASA could have attracted some of the most brilliant young people of our generation to risk their lives on a venture that might, or might not, succeed. But in response to an injunction by President Kennedy to make no small plans, NASA officials firmly declared, "We are going to send a man to the moon during the next decade. Who wants to be the first person in history to walk on the lunar surface?"

It seems that high achievers find challenge, discovery, and excitement exhilarating. Making large plans and sticking with them is what makes high achievers. It's an upward-reaching mentality. It's the kind of mentality that attracts the people who can help you reach your high goals. Of course you will be making intermediate goals to help you on your path to the top, but you must always envision the large plan as your ultimate goal.

We were created to make no small plans. If our minds were to begin to fathom the things God wants to accomplish through us, there would be no end to our excitement and enthusiasm. After all, He makes no small plans for us.

Won't you join with me right now to adopt the attitude of making no small plans *in everything you do in your life?* Let it take hold of you from this moment, and you will feel excitement, energy, and unleashed power. You will have the support of dynamic people wherever you go.

I recently saw this inscription on a plaque hanging on an office wall:

> You leave school to go out and slay a dragon
> And save the world,
> But, alas, there are no dragons,
> At least in your neighborhood
> So you wind up campaigning
> Against an occasional lizard.
> Bring on the dragons!

Have you been campaigning against lizards? Have you been wasting your life by making small plans? High achievers ought to be going for the big stuff. Bring on the dragons! Let's make no small plans!

5

High Achievers
Are Willing
To Do What They Fear

Fear is the most powerfully inhibiting force known to man. It restricts us, tightens us, and causes us to panic, forcing us to abandon our great plans of life. If we are not willing to do what we fear, then fear, not ourselves, is in control of our lives. The high achiever cannot afford to surrender control of his or her life to fear.

Fear Abounds

Psychologists tell us that fear is the most common emotion in our society today. There are six basic fears that most people have:

1. Fear of rejection or criticism
2. Fear of ill health
3. Fear of poverty

4. Fear of old age
5. Fear of the loss of a loved one—being left alone
6. Fear of death—the foundation of all fear

Unfortunately, fear's power is amplified by fear itself. It works like this: The more you fear something, the more that fear intensifies, and the more paralyzing it becomes. In many ways, worry becomes a self-fulfilling prophecy. That which we fear tends to come upon us.

Fear Wastes Potential

The poet Whittier lamented, "For all sad words of tongue or pen, the saddest are these, 'It might have been.' " The tragedy of contemporary American life is that the masses of people lead what Henry David Thoreau called, in *Walden*, "lives of quiet desperation." Far too many creative people go to their graves with songs that were never written, pictures that were never painted, businesses that were never built, troubled hearts that were never gladdened. The reason? Fear.

Many potentially high achievers never break out of the rut of mediocrity because they are intimidated by fear. High achievers simply refuse to allow fear to cause them to waste their great potential. They face it head on.

Doubt: The Twin Brother of Fear

"Our doubts are traitors and make us lose the good we oft might win," wrote Shakespeare in *Measure for*

Measure. Doubt destroys faith—faith in ourselves and in God. We lose all of the power that faith can give to us when we allow doubt, the twin brother of fear, to overwhelm us.

We live in an age that worships science. However, the very nature of science is such that it causes us to doubt anything that we cannot see, hear, smell, taste, or touch. Unfortunately, for many people this creates the kind of doubt which says that nothing is valid unless it can be proven scientifically.

There is little doubt in my mind that I'd rather live in the twentieth century than in any other period of history. I thoroughly enjoy my air-conditioned automobile, modern appliances, and communication systems. However, many of the things that make life worth living lie beyond the reach of science and technology. How do you prove love? Or courage? Or hope? Without these marvelous human attitudes and feelings, life for most of us would be worthless.

We can be open both to scientific achievement and to realities that we cannot experience with our five senses.

But when spiritual doubt takes hold of our lives, we become immobilized and cannot realize our potential. All high achievements require confidence, the antithesis of doubt and fear.

Fear Causes Us To
Hang on to False Security

Surveys have revealed that over two-thirds of all middle-aged Americans hate their jobs and wish that they could do something else. How many people do you know who are in careers that are unsatisfying to them, who work for people they dislike intensely, or who work in positions beneath their abilities? Why do so many people hang on to what they've got? Why don't they break loose and become something they have not yet been? Fear. That's why they hang on to the security of a steady income, fringe benefits, and peer approval. They may hate what they do, but they keep doing the same thing day after day, year after year, rather than face the fear of trying something else.

Perhaps you are caught in a rut like this. Maybe you have a dream you constantly long to pursue, but you hang on to the security of something solid, rather than risk loss. High achievers understand the old saying, ''It is better to try something and fail, than to try nothing and succeed.'' They'd rather take the risk of possible loss and personal agony than live with the certain misery and a sense of desperation.

Fear Wastes Our Energies

It is a common misconception that hard work is the most exhausting human activity. Actually, the greatest energy-sapper most of us ever face is emotional fatigue. And the greatest source of emotional fatigue is anxiety. I'm sure you know people who usually show up on Monday mornings looking exhausted from the weekend. They should be refreshed and full of vigor, enthusiasm, alertness, and creativity. Instead they are tired, listless, and irritable.

''What did you do this weekend?'' you ask cautiously.

''Oh, nothing much,'' comes the fatalistic response.

Then why are they so drained? The answer is probably emotional fatigue. Upon further questioning, you might discover that their "nothing much" all weekend included sitting around and worrying about something they didn't have or could lose. Their best creative energies have been wiped out by anxiety.

High achievers have learned that fear wears them out. It makes it difficult for them to relax and get the rest they need to be at their best. High achievers will not give fear the place it seeks to hold. They control fear rather than allowing fear to control them.

Fear Makes Us Pessimistic

Listening to some people talk, you'd think that nobody around them ever does anything right. But if you get behind their critical masks, you'll discover that they also feel that way about themselves. They have become so intimidated by their own feelings of inferiority that they are unable to see the good in anybody.

Fear makes us suspicious of other people, overly critical of ourselves and others, and pessimistic. It is a foolish game to believe you can raise your level of achievement by pulling down the achievements of other people. It simply doesn't work. Why not overcome the fear that causes you to be so defensive, and reach out to claim your rightful place among the high achievers of the world?

We Cannot Escape Fear

The jittery businessman, the terrified teenager, and the worried homemaker might desperately try to escape the gnawing fear that stalks them. But ultimately they are forced to admit that they simply cannot outrun what they fear. When you drink to escape misgivings about yourself and your future, those fears return as soon as you are sober, and they usually bring new fears with them. If you try to anesthetize yourself against fear by using drugs, as soon as the effect wears off, you are faced not only with those same ugly fears but also with the loss of valuable time. Attempts to escape fear are unrealistic—wherever you go, fear will follow.

Overcome Fear by Facing It

Fear almost caused me to miss two out of the most rewarding experiences of my life—witnessing the births of my two children. I have always been frightened by the sight of blood, and when my wife requested that I stay with her for the birth of our first child, I couldn't believe she was serious. But Cindy was very persuasive, and I reluctantly agreed to participate in the sessions leading up to the birth and to be present during the delivery.

As we attended the prenatal sessions, I felt my confidence beginning to build, and I became so excited that I lost sight of my fear. When time came for the delivery, I was so involved in helping Cindy with her breathing sequences that I didn't feel ill during the entire delivery process. Imagine me, the queasy one, right there sharing the glorious birth experience with Cindy.

If you don't overcome fear, the fear will control you. I would have missed one of the greatest experiences of my life if I had allowed my fear of blood to keep me in the waiting room.

How many of us settle for staying in the "waiting room" and missing out on life's great experiences? When my son was born two years later, I would not have missed his birth for anything in the world.

Fear is a Fraud

Zig Ziglar, one of America's favorite motivational speakers and authors, states that fear is an acronym standing for "False Evidence Appearing Real."

Psychologists tell us that most of our fears are false and that worrying about them is unnecessary. The following is a reliable breakdown of the time that people spend on various worries:

1. Things that will never happen 40%
2. Things that are in the past 30%
3. Needless concerns about one's health 12%
4. Petty and miscellaneous cares 10%
5. Real and legitimate concerns 8%

Of the 8 percent of the worries that are real and legitimate, half of them are about things we cannot influence. Furthermore, by taking positive steps we can eliminate about 2 percent of the real dangers we face. Therefore, it makes sense to be concerned about 2 percent of our worries.

When you understand the dynamics of fear, you can face it and conquer it.

Overcome Fear by Taking Positive Action

Courage is not the absence of fear, any more than faith is the absence of doubt. The brave soldier in combat is not the foolhardy daredevil who doesn't know what it feels like to be afraid. The one who is really brave is that soldier who does what duty demands despite his fear. That's the true nature of courage.

The real heroes, whether in war or in daily life, don't start out that way. They don't plan to demonstrate great bravery. Usually, they'd rather not be doing what they feel they must at their moment of courage. But when duty calls something within them says, You must respond.

No, courage is not the absence of fear; it is the willingness to take positive action in the face of perceived danger. Bravery is an action of the will, as opposed to a condition of the mind.

High achievers have come to understand this concept and are willing to do what they fear. For them, the credo is an old proverb, "Fear and doubt knocked on the door; courage and faith answered; there was no one there."

If you are to become a high achiever, go ahead and do what you fear. If you submit to fear's influence, it will keep you from enjoying the exhilaration of achieving high goals. If you overcome your fear, it will float away like a morning fog under the heat of the rising sun.

Challenging Your Fears

One of the greatest demonstrations of a willingness to do what you fear was exhibited by Roger Reynolds, who ran the Boston Marathon for his fourth time a couple of years ago experiencing intense pain every step of the way.

Roger has one leg that is half an inch shorter than the other, according to a story by Bill Shaw in the *Indianapolis Monthly* (November 1981). Yet despite the pain this causes him, he runs fifteen miles every morning. To grasp the full significance of this man's willingness to do what he fears, you need to know the story behind his handicap. You see, Roger's real passion is for skydiving. What really excites him is the exhilaration of falling freely through the bright Indiana sky.

In 1974, when Roger was twenty-one, he was a sergeant, a Green Beret, and a member of the U.S. Army parachute team, the "Golden Knights." He was a professional, a trained warrior, a tough kid.

On an overcast day in April, the team was in Charlottesville, Virginia, to perform in the Dogwood Festival. Despite the heavy cloud cover, the team leader decided to go ahead with the skydiving demonstration. Young Roger was to perform a dangerous stunt called "the cut-a-way," in which he was to intentionally collapse his first chute to terrify the crowd below. At the last minute he was to release the collapsed chute and pull the rip cord on his second chute, which would float him to the ground, to sighs of relief and applause from the crowd. It was a familiar routine that he had executed hundreds of times before for air shows around the world. It was his 959th jump.

Roger was not feeling well that morning, and he was mildly irritated because the weather was forcing him to perform the stunt at less than 2,000 feet (most experts considered it madness to perform at less than 5,000 feet because the margin for error is so slim). His airplane trembled and bounced in the gusts. As always, Roger shot out of the plane like a bullet, pulled the cord, and felt the reassuring lift of the chute billowing out and slowing his fall. But the comforting tug of the line was short-lived. Within a few seconds he discovered the chute was not billowing—it had collapsed. He was falling face down at more than one hundred miles per hour. Frantically, he glanced up and saw what every skydiver has nightmares about. The chute was tangled and spinning uselessly. Skydivers call it a "streamer," and it's the worst thing that can possibly happen. Don't panic, he told himself, This has happened before. He pulled on the cord to cut himself free from the collapsed parachute, but it was jammed. He pulled so hard he cut his finger to the bone, but the cord would not budge. That morning he had failed to check his equipment—a cardinal sin for any parachutist.

Now it was time for emergency action. He pulled the cord for the second chute, praying it wouldn't tangle in the first. Unfortunately, it did. He felt a wave of nausea sweep over him as the ground came toward him at a dizzying pace. This is what it feels like to die, he said to himself. Suddenly, all he could think about were his mother, father, and sisters in Indianapolis. He didn't feel so tough any more. Now he was a frightened child wanting his parents.

With a sickening crunch, Sgt. Reynolds slammed into the freshly plowed earth, breaking every major bone on his left side.

"There was a tremendous whoosh and everything went blank," he later remembered. When he regained consciousness he saw that blood-stained bones poked through his blue-and-gold jumpsuit, his foot was twisted backward, and with the slightest movement he could hear his bones grating against each other. People were standing around talking about how lucky he was to be alive. But he didn't feel lucky.

At the hospital, the doctors predicted he would die—or at best be crippled for life. The odds against his walking again were a thousand to one. And it was obvious even to a layman that he would never run.

Roger spent sixteen months in the hospital—plenty long enough to have nightmares about the great fear that welled up inside him. The day he left the hospital, he couldn't stand up straight, was fifty pounds thinner, and walked painfully with a cane. But Roger knew what he had to do. Shortly after he left the hospital, he climbed into an airplane and took and passed his pilot's test. For sixteen months he had been sidelined, recovering in a hospital, and he had used the time to prepare for the test. With that intermediate goal accomplished, he set about to conquer the greatest fear he had. He drove back home to Indiana, to a parachute-drop zone where he had learned to skydive as a high school kid.

No one expected it of him—at least no one but himself. His friends shook their heads and said he was crazy. They backed away, refusing to have any part in his "death jump." They tried to reason with him, "Your body is weakened from being laid up." "You don't have the strength to survive." "You can't even stand up, much less jump from an airplane." "Your leg will shatter into a hundred pieces." But Roger ignored the sensible advice, struggled into the airplane, and checked his equipment—twice.

"I had to conquer that fear," he later told a reporter. "I was afraid, but when I jumped, the fear was gone. At three thousand feet, the world was as beautiful and breathtaking as I had remembered.''

His friends tried to soften his impact. They grabbed a blanket and ran to hold it like a fire net so he wouldn't shatter his legs again. But Roger waved them away. He landed on his one good leg. He had done it!

This courageous young man, who was told he would probably never walk again—much less run—began to jog to try to regain his athletic conditioning. At first, the pain was unbearable—he couldn't run to the end of the driveway. But he pushed himself, and within a few days he was forcing his legs to carry him around the block. On he went, around the next block—a mile, two miles, three miles, on and on, every day. But even after running for several years, he still felt excruciating pain.

In 1978, without telling anyone, Roger boarded a train in Indianapolis and traveled to Boston. There he entered and ran the Boston Marathon. Although he wasn't on the program as an official entrant and he didn't even have a number to prove he'd run, *he* knew he'd done it, and that was all that mattered.

He's run four twenty-six-mile marathons since that time, and he has kept on jumping from airplanes. Recently, Roger bought some mountaineering equipment; he eventually plans to climb the Himalayas. He's also planning to be an orthopedic surgeon someday. He would like to put together bones that have been shattered, as his were. He's a rare breed, a high achiever, a person who is willing to do what he fears.

No one has to tell Roger Reynolds that his achievements are great. He knows, and that's all that matters. In fact, Roger resists the limelight and feels embarrassed when people talk about how brave he is. For him, he's simply one man taking on the sky, the mountain, the ocean, the medical books, the pain, and life itself.

The High Achiever's Action Plan

What fears are holding you back from great achievement in your life? What great and mighty goals might you attempt to reach, had you no fear? True motivation for the high achiever can only occur when fear is replaced. But replaced with what?

Fear can only be replaced with confidence. The word confidence comes from the Latin phrase *con fideo*, meaning "with faith." Fear is replaced with faith—faith in who you are, faith in your life's purpose, faith in where you are going. Don't be afraid to climb out of the rut. A truly interesting life is not possible without some risk.

Sit down and make a list of all the things you are afraid to do, within legal, moral, and spiritual limits. Then go out and deliberately make yourself do every one of them. Each time you confront fear, become sensitive to the atmosphere surrounding it. Keep your senses fully open to receive and record even the smallest details. Don't let fear block your sensory resources. Make a conscious effort to observe everything around you. By concentrating on the atmosphere in this way, you may be able to ward off the intimidation of the task ahead.

If you are to become a high achiever, you must be willing to transcend fear. If you step out and are willing to do what you fear, then fear will no longer control your life. You will be on your way to high achievement.

6

High Achievers Are Willing To Prepare

Twenty lightning-fast minutes. That's all my guide Alfons Franzen allowed for my celebration after reaching the top of the Matterhorn. Was I disappointed? Did I feel cheated? Indeed not! That brief interlude, which lasted five minutes more than a typical coffee break, was the culmination of years of planning, hard work, and preparation. It was my personal confirmation that it had all been worthwhile. You see, high achievers learn early in the game that the exhilaration of attaining high goals is not as great as the constant joy of achieving progressively higher intermediate goals in the daily experience of preparation. They learn that high achievement is a process rather than an event. They soon come to know that every big event is a direct result of many little events that have been carefully planned and faithfully implemented along the way.

Once you have reached a high goal, you can talk
about it, write about it, and savor it as a memory. But
high achievers get more excited about what they are
becoming than what they have done.

Accomplishments Look Easy

Have you ever watched the Olympic ice skaters as they
gracefully perform their routines to the rhythm of
beautiful music? They always make it look so easy.
Every movement is fluid, every step carefully calculated
to add something to the drama of the presentation.
Even their expressions help you capture the mood of
their routines. In fact, high achievers in almost every
field of endeavor have a way of making their achievements look easy to the uninitiated. The skilled orators,
the great musicians, the poised business leaders, the outstanding athletes—all usually leave you with the feeling,
I could do that!

Quick-flash inspirations are a dime a dozen. The line
from the old song *Pretend* is true, "Remember anyone
can dream." But the difference between dreaming and
high achievement is a lot of hard work and preparation.
The failure to achieve high goals is, in most cases, due
not so much to a lack of ability as to an unwillingness to
prepare. It is always easier to rationalize your failures
away than to go through the struggle of preparation.

A Word About Luck

In the corporate world, there's an old saying that is often used by disgruntled individuals who have a way of noticing how quickly relatives of company officials progress: "It's a lot easier to climb the ladder of success when your daddy holds the ladder!" There is little question that good fortune has played a big part in the success of many. An aspiring actress always has a much better chance of succeeding if she happens to be beautiful. The son of a wealthy and successful businessman usually has a greater chance of stepping into a higher position early in his career. Who would deny that some people always chance to be in the right place at the right time?

The story is told of a successful businessman who was given a testimonial dinner by the grateful citizens of the city to which he had contributed so much. In introducing the much-revered man, the mayor of the city listed his many achievements, including being president of the largest bank in the city, having vast holdings in real estate, being chairman of the boards of many of the town's leading corporations, and having made a host of civic contributions.

"Most of you know," said the honored man when he began to speak, "the things that I have accomplished during my twenty years in this city. What you may not know is that when I came to this town, all I owned were the clothes on my back and the contents of a small grocery bag."

"What was in the bag?" a young man asked at the close of the speech.

"A million dollars worth of stocks I had inherited from my grandfather," was the reply.

Most of us would like to have started with such an endowment. Most of us would like to be a lot luckier than we appear to be. However, most of us let more good fortune slip through our fingers every day than we could ever use in a lifetime. Isn't it true that few of us ever do everything that we can with the opportunities and resources we have?

There is a way to increase our percentage of lucky breaks. It's expressed in the following statement: "I've noticed that the harder I work, the luckier I get!" I'm also fond of this wise anonymous saying: "Good fortune is what happens when opportunity meets with preparation." Thomas A. Edison said it this way: "He profiteth, who hustles while he waits."

The difference between high achievers and "also-rans" is almost always the degree of preparation. It's this simple: If you want to become a high achiever, preparation must become a way of life—every single day of your existence. Of the six attitudes I listed that are characteristic of high achievers, this one is the most crucial.

You Were Born a Planner

Everything about the universe around us speaks of careful planning and order. As a creature made in the image of God you were given the ability to arrange your life and to affect your environment.

I guess by now you have discovered that I consider Jesus to be the greatest person who ever lived. In my estimation, He was the highest achiever in history, and He was also a great planner. Consider for a moment the overwhelming nature of the task He faced. He was given only thirty-three years to alter dramatically the course of history. Yet He never seemed confused about what He was going to do next, nor did He waste His energies on worthless tasks. He carefully planned what He would do, and set about His tasks with complete commitment and confidence.

These characteristics have applied to all the great achievers of history. Even the people we consider to have been the most creative have been habitual planners. Leonardo da Vinci invested his most creative energies and efforts in planning. Historians tell us that the great da Vinci would often spend years drawing the plans for a magnificent painting. And then, once he had completed the plans, he would give them to his students to finish. He was such a great planner that once his work was laid out even people less skilled than he could execute his plans. You, too, were born to plan.

What Is Planning?

"Organizing is what you do before you do something so that when you do it, it's not all mixed up," said that great philosopher, Christopher Robin, in A.A. Milne's *Winnie the Pooh.*

The concept of planning frightens many people. To some it means putting themselves into a straitjacket. To others the idea of planning is threatening because they think it restricts their creativity and spontaneity. Still others view it as a useless activity. For them, all that matters is action. They are a little like a drowning man who splashes furiously in the water. He may work feverishly and become dangerously exhausted, but all this activity cannot save him.

Losers always concentrate on activities, but high achievers concentrate on planning and making every movement count in their efforts to reach progressively higher intermediate goals.

So what is planning? My working definition is as follows: Planning is a careful selection and systematic arrangement of progressively higher intermediate goals leading to a high goal. Planning is as simple as deciding what you're going to do and how you're going to do it—before you begin. And the better your plan, the more likely you are to reach your ultimate goal.

Isn't it amazing how many people, though they would not dare to start out on a trip across America without a carefully charted course, will spend all their lives without a plan for the future?

Three Basic Elements of Preparation

Good preparation always includes three elements: mastery of technical skills, building endurance, and gaining confidence. To reach your high goal, you must first plan how you will master the necessary technical skills. Thomas Carlyle once remarked in *Sartor Resartus*, "Man is a tool-using animal. . . . Without tools he is nothing, with tools he is all." Those are the words worth remembering.

Every area of human activity has its unique tools. Those tools might be words, surgical instruments, computers, budgets, or machinery, but they are the implements that are necessary to accomplish skillfully the task at hand. Mastery of technical skills includes learning what tools are available to do the best job and how to use those tools with dexterity. Also, there are techniques and short cuts that have been developed by experts in every area of activity. Learning those techniques and short cuts is high on the priority list for those who would become high achievers. But it is never enough to become simply good at using the techniques and tools of a particular pursuit. The high achiever always seeks to become a master of those skills.

Arthur Rubinstein once astounded a young inquirer with the statement that he practiced piano eight hours a day, every day of his life.

"But, sir!" exclaimed the young man, "You are so good. Why do you practice so much?"

"I wish to become superb," replied the master pianist.

Many people are good at the technical skills of their particular activity, but life's high achievers always seek to become superb.

Secondly, preparation includes building endurance. As you plan your preparation, be sure to include plans for conditioning yourself to be able to keep going when everything within you is screaming for you to stop.

When I was trying to convince my wife to join me in climbing Mount Kilimanjaro, she resisted, reading me quotes from newspaper articles and magazines on the rigors of high altitude climbing. Both she and I knew that if we were to climb that 19,340-foot mountain successfully, we had to condition ourselves to endure intense pain. That kind of endurance could only be achieved through careful preparation. After she agreed, our first priority was to plan an orderly system of getting ourselves in shape.

Thirdly, good preparation always includes building confidence. Most of us enjoy doing whatever we do well. Why? Because we have adequately prepared ourselves, and we are confident that we can do whatever is required.

For example, high achievers in the sales field prepare themselves so well that whenever they make a pitch they are virtually flawless. They have made the pitch so many times that it has become second nature to them.

If you are to become a high achiever in any field, make sure you build your confidence. That way, you will do your best.

The Importance of Struggle

In the world of business, I have noticed that the high achievers are seldom the people who breezed through school with straight A's. School work usually came easy to these A students. As a result, they learned a lot of information and techniques to pass tests.

More often, the high achievers in almost any field of endeavor are the people who had to work for the A's, B's and C's. Most of these A, B, and C students found school difficult. In order to survive in the academic environment, they had to learn how to study. They also learned something else that was very important—they learned how to *struggle*.

If you want to become a high achiever, you must learn how to struggle against the obstacles that get in your way. High achievers seldom refer to obstacles they encounter as "unexpected delays" or "developments." The expect to encounter resistance along the way and condition themselves to face delays and obstacles without discouragement.

Preparation Includes Self-Discipline

It is always easier not to prepare than to force yourself through the rigors of preparation. When I decided to begin running long distances, I discovered that getting started is the toughest part. It is always easier to roll over and go back to sleep, especially before the sun comes up or on a Saturday, than it is to rise and go out into the freezing cold and begin your long run. The greatest enemy of preparation is procrastination. As long as you struggle with the "I'll start tomorrow" mentality you will never overcome the obstacles along the way.

Procrastination is a nasty habit, usually cultivated over a lifetime, that steals away the greatest opportunities of life. Yet it is a habit that most of us have developed through failure to discipline ourselves. Many books have been written about breaking the procrastination habit, but most of us have put off reading them or, having read them, have decided not to respond to their advice. I have found that the only successful way to break the procrastination habit is to cultivate the reverse habit. A habit is nothing more than an action you have taken so many times that it has become automatic to you. Just as you can procrastinate so often that it becomes habitual, you can refuse to procrastinate often enough that *that* becomes an automatic response. Unless you cultivate this "nonprocrastination" habit you will never become a high achiever.

Another very good habit to cultivate is to do something every day that will prepare you for your high goal. At first these daily tasks might be very small, but as you build momentum you will be able to increase your preparation time each day. Also, you'll find that as you step out to become a high achiever, discouragement will tempt you. The only way to overcome it is to take an immediate step toward reaching your goal every single day.

Cultivate Self-Control as a Way of Life

Each of us has only one real freedom, but it is our freedom and no one can take it away from us. We cannot control what happens to us, or what people do to us, or where we start in the race of life. But we *can* control how we react to our experiences. We can allow circumstances to bury us, or we can choose to rise above them and become high achievers.

A young man once told Dr. Norman Vincent Peale, the great minister and motivational speaker, that he wanted to start his own business but did not have any money. "Empty pockets never held anyone back," was Dr. Peale's response, "only empty heads and empty hearts can do that!"

Exercising self-control means that you take charge of your own life, as opposed to letting external circumstances and events govern your life. Many of the people with whom I talk feel that they have very little control over their lives. They work under a boss who is a tyrant, they live with a domineering mate, or they feel that their finances place heavy restrictions upon them. It is true for most of us that there are many things over which we have little influence. However, it is also true that it doesn't take much control to change the entire course of our lives. Skilled sea captains, for example, know that there are many overwhelming forces that control the movement of the giant ocean liner they must take across the sea, particularly in stormy weather. They are controlled by the weight of the ship, the movement and mass of the water, and the force of the wind. However, they also know that by turning the relatively small rudder only a degree or two at precisely the right moment, they can alter the ultimate destination of the ship by as much as a thousand miles.

Sometimes, as you set out to prepare yourself for high achievement, it seems as if everything around you is conspiring to keep you from reaching your high goal. But years of preparation, struggle, and exercise of self-control have taught me that there is a certain rhythm and harmony to life. The secret is to pick up on that rhythm and harmony and take advantage of the momentum it gives you, rather than fight against the elements you feel are seeking to control your life. Remember what St. Francis of Assisi said: "God grant me the serenity to accept the things I cannot change, the courage to change the things I can, and the wisdom to know the difference."

Cultivating self-control also means that you refuse to allow the opinions of others to direct you. Their opinions can affect you in two ways: (1) the flattery of people can make you lazy and self-satisfied, and (2) the disparaging remarks of others can discourage you and destroy your confidence. High achievers have learned to exercise self-control by ignoring flattery and weighing, not counting, their critics.

Exercising Your Will

The natural resistance to the rigors of preparation can only be conquered by exercising your will. "But I don't have any willpower,'' many people complain. One reason most people have such weak wills is that they refuse to exercise them, and their wills become flabby, weak, and ineffective. Just as your body has to be conditioned, your will must also be conditioned in order for you to achieve. It's simple: The more you exercise your will, the stronger it becomes.

In 1976, Indiana University's basketball team was undefeated throughout the regular season and captured the NCAA National Championship under the tutelage of its great coach, Bobby Knight. Shortly thereafter, Coach Knight was interviewed on the television show "60 Minutes." The commentator asked him, "Why is it, Bobby, that your basketball teams at Indiana are always so successful? Is it the will to succeed?"

"The will to succeed is important," replied Bobby Knight, "but I'll tell you what's more important—it's the will to prepare. It's the will to go out there every day training and building those muscles and sharpening those skills!" Non achievers are driven by the desire for immediate gratification and seek to escape struggle at every opportunity. All great achievements are the result of work and patient endurance.

"As we sow, so shall we reap," says Christ in his Sermon on the Mount. What we'll reap tomorrow, we must sow today through preparation.

The masters of every art, sport, or skill make their feats look easy. Through long and arduous preparation, they have developed their technical skills and mental conditioning to the point that their actions have become natural responses. Not everyone can climb fast, but anyone can climb high. The high achiever learns to enjoy the climb because he or she knows that preparation is the path to great accomplishment.

In closing this chapter, let me share with you the amazing and paradoxical secrets every high achiever must know:

1. It takes less energy to keep on climbing than to stop and hang on a ledge.
2. It takes less energy to go for the top than to wallow in the valley of frustration and anguish.
3. It's easier to contribute to life than to lie around.
4. It's easier to grow than to decay.
5. It's easier to prepare than to procrastinate.

Peak performance is exhilarating and exciting! The moment you begin your preparation, you will experience tremendous energy, and each step will take you nearer to the ultimate accomplishment of your high goal.

7

High Achievers Are Willing To Risk Failure

Thomas J. Watson, long-time president of IBM, has a simple formula for achieving success: Double your failure rate. The idea of succeeding by doubling your failure rate might sound strange to you. However, if you are going to be a high achiever, you must learn how to "fail" your way to high achievement. Failing successfully is the only way to the top. Failure is not the enemy of success. It is a teacher—a harsh teacher, but the best!

Failure can either be a weight, or it can give you wings. In the 1952 Olympic games Milt Campbell was the silver medalist behind gold medal winner Bob Mathias in the decathlon. Four years later Milt Campbell won the gold medal for that event and Rafer Johnson won the silver. Four years later Rafer Johnson won the gold medal and C. K. Yang won the silver. Again, C. K. Yang won the gold medal on his next try, and broke the world's record for the decathlon.

Failure is a great character-builder. It can give you strength to run and stamina to climb. I don't know of any high achiever who has not gone through the depths of failure. The secret is to learn from your failures. Every job has its share of problems and frustrations. High achievers recognize this as a fact of life and don't let disappointments stop them in their efforts.

See if you can identify one of the greatest people of history by a record of failures:

- 1832, lost his job and was defeated for the legislature
- 1833, failed in business
- 1835, lost his sweetheart to death
- 1836, had a nervous breakdown
- 1838, was defeated for Speaker of Congress
- 1843, was defeated in bid for Congress
- 1848, was again defeated in bid for Congress
- 1849, was rejected for Land Officer
- 1854, was defeated for Senate
- 1856, lost nomination for Vice Presidency
- 1858, was again defeated in Senate race.

Perhaps you would recognize this person as one of the truly great leaders of America—Abraham Lincoln.

Lincoln had a reputation for never giving less than his best in any undertaking, even in the face of overwhelming problems, disappointments, and setbacks. As a young man he vowed: "I will always try to do my best no matter what . . . and someday my chance will come." He did his best, his chance came, and he took his rightful place among the greatest high achievers in history.

A Revolutionary Concept

This idea may sound unconventional—even revolutionary. It may conflict with everything you have ever been taught. But if taken seriously, it could seriously change your way of dealing with opportunities.

Here is a phrase you may have heard throughout your life: Anything worth doing, is worth doing well. But the high achiever says: Anything worth doing, is worth doing badly—at least at first. That first step upward toward your high achievement is the most difficult. It is the step most people will never take because they might not do it well the first time or even the second. To become a high achiever you must be willing to do it badly at first, and trust that improvements will follow.

When I first started climbing mountains, I did it badly. When I first started speaking to groups, I did it badly. When I first started selling my company's cleaning services, I did it badly. But through persistence, I have become better at doing all of these things.

Failing My Way to Success

Failure plagued me during my first two years in business. Not only was the company losing money, but as the only salesman I was responsible for bringing in new customers. Each day I would go out and call on industrial plants and commercial buildings to see if we could be of service to them. I must have been doing it badly because I even had trouble making small sales.

There was, however, one prospective customer in the Indianapolis area that I had intentionally avoided calling. I would often think about this possible client, but I neglected to call because I didn't feel that my company was well enough established to make a successful sale. I didn't want to fail.

That prospective customer was the Indianapolis Motor Speedway, the home of the Indianapolis 500. Ever since my father had taken me to my first race, the 500-mile race had held a mystical aura for me. How wonderful it would be to have the Indianapolis Motor Speedway as one of my clients. But I could not make that opening sales call. What if they didn't want me? What would I do if I failed? Should I wait for another year, and get more experience? No, I finally told myself, I'm going out to the Speedway today. I'll try, even if I do it badly.

What happened at the Indianapolis Motor Speedway that day is a classic story of "failing" your way to success. It is a typical story of the development of a salesman and a young company. To a large extent, our company's ultimate success resulted from what happened that day at the Indianapolis Motor Speedway.

I got up that morning at 6:30, looked out the window and saw a blue, cloudless, early spring sky. On my desk at the office was a piece of paper with the telephone number of the Indianapolis Motor Speedway and the name of the man who was in charge of maintenance and facilities, Mr. Clarence Cagle. I shuddered when I picked up that piece of paper and looked at the name of a man who was one of the world's experts on racing track surfaces.

At 8:00 I forced myself to call his number. His secretary answered, and I told her who I was and that I wanted to speak with Mr. Cagle concerning a new heavy-duty cleaning service I had started. She checked and told me that Mr. Cagle would see me at 2:00 that afternoon. I hung up the phone and breathed a huge sigh of relief. This initial victory felt so great, I wished I could have contented myself with that success, rather than risk the possibility of rejection that afternoon.

Like any good salesman, I headed out to the racetrack extra early and took a tour around the track. I found three major heavy-duty cleaning needs, and I was confident I could win over Mr. Cagle.

At 2:00 I entered Mr. Cagle's office. He shook my hand, sat down behind his desk, and asked what I was selling. Now it was my turn. I told him I had a new company and we did heavy-duty cleaning that used high-pressure hot water and chemicals. I reviewed what I had seen on the bus tour and confidently stated to him, "You know those squiggly tire marks that the race cars leave on the track when they spin out and those black smears on the white concrete wall where their magnesium tires hit and sometimes cause flash fires? Well," I continued, "that's got to be psychologically defeating for the other drivers to look at as they drive at high speeds close to those walls. We could come out here each night with our cleaning equipment and wash off the tire marks and black smudges. We could also wash off the heavy oil and tire residue that builds up in the grooves through the corners and becomes slick and dangerous for the drivers."

"Young man," he spoke softly but firmly, "you cannot touch this track with anything artificial or the USAC, the sanctioning body, and this speedway could be sued for everything we've got. Only Mother Nature is allowed to wash the track's surface."

Strike one. But I wasn't finished. "Well, Mr. Cagle," I replied, "we could clean up all the oil and grease in those garages back in Gasoline Alley where the crews work on the race cars."

"Young man, those garages are immaculate. The minute a drop of oil hits the floor, a mechanic is there with a rag to wipe it up."

Strike two. But before losing any hope of ever having the Indianapolis Motor Speedway as a client, I became a truly professional salesman. I used a technique of selling that has been invaluable in developing our cleaning services into a successful company today. It is the basic technique of consultive selling. I simply looked him directly in the eyes, didn't make any further assertions, and humbly asked him, "Do you have any cleaning problems?"

With that question, his interest in our conversation picked up noticeably. He motioned for me to come outside with him. "See that?" he asked, as he pointed up and down the length of the upper and lower grandstands along the one-mile straightaway and well into the first turn. "That's my biggest cleaning problem—cleaning all those folding metal chairs every year. If you could figure out a better way to do it, you'd have a job out here every year."

Then he explained how those metal chairs sit out all year accumulating dirt. Every year the speedway hired forty to fifty labor-pool people from downtown, gave them water buckets, rags, and sponges, and put one man in each row to wipe down each individual chair. The process took over a month, and the quality of the cleaning was terrible.

The following day I brought our new pressure-cleaning truck out to the speedway and did a test. It was much faster than the old way, and the quality was excellent. He hired us. We did the job in eight days with four men and our truck. The speedway was thrilled. Every year since then, we've cleaned the chairs and also done other projects for them. Our credibility with our contacts in manufacturing plants immediately soared because the Indianapolis Motor Speedway was one of our clients. Today our company is a multi-million-dollar cleaning-management service and contracting company with more than two hundred of the largest manufacturing and utility industry clients in the United States.

The speedway was my first high achievement in my new business, and it launched even higher achievements —simply because one April day I made up my mind that I was willing to fail.

How many people do you know who could have been outstanding leaders but who have settled for middle or lower positions because they dared not risk failure? How many athletes do you know who had the potential for being outstanding business, community, or spiritual leaders, who stopped striving after successful high school, college, or professional sports careers because they dared not face the possibility of failing in a different field?

Take a look at your own life. Is there a dream that has haunted you from childhood? One which you have not pursued because you have not been willing to risk failure? Have you continued working at a job you detest because it provides security, rather than reaching out to start your own business, get a better job, or further your education? There is no time like the present to gather up courage and pursue the goals you have dreamed of.

When a Failure is Not a Failure

You have only failed when you have failed to try. If you learn something valuable from your failure—if you develop strength of character—you can use it as a stepping stone along the road to high achievement.

Failures and disappointments put us under a great deal of pressure, but they also bring out strength, character, and endurance vital to high achievement. As an old proverb says: "A diamond is a chunk of coal that made good under pressure."

8

High Achievers Are Teachable

To reach high goals, you must be teachable. Perhaps there is no one who has achieved the specific high goal you are pursuing, and you may be alone on some parts of the journey. There will, however, be many people along the way who can help you to climb more easily and effectively.

The person who is not teachable is doomed to repeat mistakes of the past. Such a person does not successfully climb the mountains of life but wanders around aimlessly in the foothills of confusion and frustration.

"Boss, I don't understand," an old employee said to his supervisor. "You have promoted three men during the last year, and I have more than twenty years of experience in this job."

"No, Charlie," the supervisor replied, "you have been in that job twenty years, but you do not have twenty years of experience. You have one year of experience twenty times because, despite my instructions, you are repeating the same mistakes you made when you first started.''

Charlie's life was nothing but a series of reruns of past failures. What a tragedy—he was locked into a job, a job from which he would never escape, because he was not teachable; he was not willing to learn as he went along.

I will never forget the best lesson in teachability I ever received. One day, the president of a meat-packing company I worked for called me into his office and informed me that my abrasive manner had alienated everyone in the company. He gave me two months termination notice. I promptly changed my attitude toward the people around me, apologized to my associates, and continued to work for that company for two more years. I became teachable.

Several years later, when I was negotiating a management service contract with a new client, I was asked to meet with the executives of that company to see if we could work together satisfactorily.

''What would you say is your greatest strength?'' one of the executives asked me.

''I think my greatest strength is that I am teachable.''

That evaluation must have impressed the prospective client, because the executives agreed to work with us. That experience made me think about how important it is to be willing to learn.

What Is Teachability?

Teachability is an openness to learn from every opportunity. Anthropologists tell us that one of the most significant differences between man and animals is that human beings have a more sophisticated learning capacity and can pass their learning on to succeeding generations. Man can collect and store information, draw conclusions, and devise a variety of ways to apply the stored information. What a wonderful God-given gift!

But it's all a matter of teachability. We can either open our minds to new information, or we can close them and refuse to take advantage of our tremendous learning capabilities. Leading neurologists have noted that the average human being has the ability to learn at least fifty foreign languages, store information contained within all of the books in a major university library, and think faster than high-speed computers. What causes us to operate at a much lower level is our unwillingness to invest what it takes to become completely open to learning.

The Urge To Imitate

Psychologists tell us that human beings have an overwhelming urge to imitate others. Either consciously or unconsciously, we look for role models after which to pattern our lives.

When I was three years old I had a friend whose nickname was "Bump." He was six years old at the time. Bump was my hero; I wanted to be like him. Everything he did I thought was great. He could ride a bike, play ball, and run well. Nobody dared to oppose Bump. Without realizing it, I observed Bump's every move. Soon I walked and talked like him and I mimicked his every action. The problem with my imitation of Bump was that I sought to *adopt* his way of life. My goal was to become like him. In the process, I began to lose my own identity. .

Far too many people are satisfied to adopt the behavior of their hero and end up acting just like him or her. It's better to *adapt* the principles of our heroes and use them as models in our lives.

Some twenty years later, I finished graduate school and accepted a mangement training position with the meatpacking company I mentioned earlier. There I was exposed to many middle- and upper-level managers. Quite consciously, I identified with one manager whom I admired. I sought to learn everything I could by watching his every action. .

This man, Rod Stephens, became my management hero. He was widely respected in the industry as a man who was always able to get things done. So I studied him. After several months he was transferred and placed in charge of an unprofitable subsidiary that had been acquired by the parent company. Much to my delight, he asked me to join him as a part of the new management team designed to make that subsidiary profitable again. I was thrilled to have this opportunity to work more closely with Rod Stephens.

During the next two years I had many occasions to watch him as he handled tough union grievance meetings, conducted weekly managers' meetings, made changes, sought to improve attitudes, and took charge of the subsidiary. I watched everything he did. Later, when faced with a challenging situation, I'd imagine how Rod Stephens would handle it, and I'd try to act accordingly. From observing Rod, I learned valuable management skills. However, I've long realized that I am an individual and must apply these admirable principles in my own way. I must adapt what I learn from my mentors, not adopt their behavior.

How Teachable Are You?: An Exercise

In my company's management development seminars, we've often used a simple exercise to find out how teachable people are. Try this exercise by yourself or with a small group. The results can be quite humorous. This is a timed exercise—you have only three minutes to complete it.

Exercise Instructions

1. Read these directions carefully before you do anything else.
2. Print your name in the upper right corner of this page.
3. Write the words "high achiever" under your name.
4. Draw five small squares in the upper left corner of this page.
5. Put an "X" in each of the squares.
6. Put a circle around each of the squares.
7. Say your name out loud.
8. In the left margin of this page multiply 777 by 33.
9. Draw a triangle around your answer.
10. If you have carefully followed instructions write "I have" in the top center of this page. Or, if you're in a group, say "I have" out loud.

11.　Now that you finished reading everything, ignore all instructions except #1.

Answer

Did you read the directions before you did anything, as you were instructed to do? If so, your page should be blank and you should have had more than enough time to complete the exercise.

If you are one of the many who completed each instruction one by one, I hope you had fun and don't feel too badly about not being perfectly teachable. Whether or not you successfully followed the instructions, I hope the point is clear. Most of us could save ourselves a lot of missed communication by being more alert, aware, and teachable. As a high achiever, you will be able to reach your high goals with fewer slip-ups if you aggressively work at developing your teachability.

How Do You Become Teachable?

In this country we have a tendency to divide life into certain stages. We think of our childhood and young adulthood as the period for learning. During that time we attend school, study various subjects, and are encouraged to get as complete an education as possible. Once we graduate, we imagine that our education is over and that we no longer need to be teachable.

Fortunately, this attitude is beginning to give way to the idea of continuing education. It is becoming more and more common for adults to take time out from their business and family activities to attend school at night, and sometimes to take years out to pursue a major course of study. It is not unusual to hear about a grand-mother, well into her eighties, who has just graduated from college. The following are some pointers that can help you become more teachable.

Have a Definite Plan for Learning

Do you have a plan for acquiring new knowledge? Are you constantly educating yourself, broadening your interests, and generating new enthusiasm? Do you pursue new avenues of adventure in your work and personal life? All of us need excitement and diversity. We need a definite, highly personalized system of learning.

The slogan of the United Negro College Fund states: "A mind is a terrible thing to waste." Unfortunately, many people who live by a strict diet plan, maintain a regular system of physical exercise, and operate their business in a very orderly fashion give very little attention to their plans for developing their minds.

The time you spend developing and executing a consistent, thorough plan for improving your mind will be some of the best you will ever invest.

Learn from People

I am convinced that human beings are influenced more by other humans than they are by abstract ideas. You can learn from the people around you as well as from the great personalities of history—if you are willing to remain teachable. Of course, teachability is not gullibility. It is important both to choose your teachers and guides carefully and to listen once you have chosen them.

A wise manager I once met advised, "Surround yourself with people who are smarter than you are." High achievers always look for and appreciate people who have more knowledge than they, who have developed outstanding skills, and who have the wisdom to apply their knowledge.

Only little minds are intimidated by great minds. The smarter a person is, the more impressed he or she usually is with the intelligence of others.

Use All Your Faculties for Learning

Learning is an active process that can best be carried out by paying attention. If you are to become a high achiever, keep active in three important ways:

1. Read. The writings and biographies of great people offer a lot of useful information and can be quite inspirational. It is too easy and tempting for people to spend hours in front of a television watching programs mindlessly. High achievers usually prefer to spend time with books that the general public doesn't read. Many towns in America have libraries that contain more books than the average person reads in a lifetime. Yet not many people take advantage of the wonderful freedom we have in this country to enjoy reading anything we choose.

2. Observe. Too many people are more concerned about other people's observations of themselves than they are about observing others. If you are to develop a

teachable spirit, become a keen observer of everything and everybody around you.

3. Listen. When the late President Lyndon B. Johnson was a junior senator from Texas, he kept a plaque on the wall in his office: "You ain't learnin' nothin' when you're doin' all the talkin'." Ralph Waldo Emerson said it more poetically in his essay *Intellect*: "Every man's progress is through a succession of teachers." You will meet many people from whom you can learn—if you take the time and trouble to listen.

Enemies of Teachability

Pride. Perhaps the most common enemy of a teachable spirit, pride blinds a person to the valuable input he or she could receive when making plans and decisions. It breeds ignorance, self-centeredness, and an attitude that ignores the good advice of others. Certainly, we should always weigh carefully any counsel we receive. It is, of course, foolish to accept the advice of unworthy teachers and unwise to take seriously every person's opinion. However, it is equally foolish to be so full of pride that you cannot receive guidance from anyone.

Skepticism and cynicism. The skeptic doubts everything that he or she is told or reads regardless of who says it. There is a point beyond which questioning of ideas and information becomes a tremendous barrier to learning. The high achiever questions information from questionable sources, but is open to information and ideas that come from reliable sources.

Lack of time. It takes time to read, to listen, and to assimilate all the information available to us. The person who is so busy acting on what he or she already knows that there is no time to receive new information is likely to go around in circles. High achievers learn to take time out for broadening their knowledge and deepening their wisdom.

The Higher You Go, The More Help You Need

An unalterable fact of high achievement is that the higher up you go, the more teachable you need to be. A highly skilled brain surgeon, for example, needs to be open to new information. Practically each day new discoveries are made that help the brain surgeon become more effective. It is only when a person of such high achievement is willing to learn continuously that he or she can develop even greater skills.

The higher you set your goals, the more help you'll need from expert guides in the field of your endeavor. The greatest athletes in the world surround themselves with coaches, managers, and other athletes who help them learn more about their sport. Likewise, salespeople, executives, professionals, artists, public speakers, and high achievers of all pursuits rely on people who can help them improve in their fields.

If you are to be great, you must be teachable. And if you are teachable, you may be called great by those around you.

9

High Achievers Have Heart

High achievers have heart. They have a single-minded purpose that they pursue regardless of cost.

At the beginning of this book, I wrote of my tremendous struggles in climbing to the peak of the Matterhorn. But I have saved a part of that story until now. It is one of my great examples of high achievement. What I didn't tell you is that it took me three attempts to make it to the top. Twice my guide and I had to turn back because of heavy snowstorms. My vacation was almost over, my train was to leave the next day for Geneva, and my wife Cindy was to meet me in Paris for our flight home. My heart was still on the mountain, but my head was telling me it was a hopeless cause.

The storms looked as if they had settled in for a few more days, and the possibility of a climb seemed to be slipping farther and farther away. I don't think I have ever been as depressed as I was that evening while eating my supper alone in the restaurant.

Questions raced through my mind. Had I wasted all

the preparation that had brought me to this point? Would I ever be this physically fit again? Could I ever afford to leave my business for three weeks to make another attempt at climbing this mountain? Could I ever again afford it financially?

I thought about an English woman I had met the previous day, who had to return home, unsuccessful in her attempt to scale the Matterhorn. It was her fifth summer of trying—she had been "weathered-out" each time. I began to hear the voices of everyone who thought I was crazy for wanting to climb the Matterhorn saying, You shouldn't be wasting time and money on this impossible project!

Lord, I prayed silently, Give me a sign of what You want me to do.

As I walked out of the restaurant, I looked up into the sky and all I saw was stars. No clouds! I rushed to a phone and called Alfons. He agreed that surprisingly it didn't look too bad, but said that we'd have to wait until morning to know for sure.

I was up early the next morning. Sure enough, the sky was clear. We could make one more attempt if I would cancel my flight home and stay. But my wife was to meet me in Paris that day for our flight home. What was I to do?

Then the *heart* of the high achiever took over as I realized that this could be my last and best chance to climb a mountain as magnificent as the Matterhorn. I pushed aside all my doubts and decided that I would take one more shot at making that climb. I called my wife's hotel in London and left a message for her to fly home without me and explain to my parents, our kids, and my employees that I had made the decision to stay and climb the Matterhorn.

The great rewards of life come to those with the heart

to persist and the courage to step away from the pessimistic crowd.

Circumstances Will Try To Hold You Back

Murphy was right: If anything can go wrong, it will go wrong. Conflict is rooted in the plots of all good short stories, novels, and movies. The old man battling against the sea, the young person struggling against tremendous physical handicaps, and the athlete working against overwhelming odds—all have the heart essential for overcoming adversity.

Why do you suppose that stories involving intense conflict are so attractive to us? Perhaps it is because all of us have experienced the weight of circumstances trying to hold us back as we battle to reach our highest goals.

A young woman named Wilma understood how circumstances try to hold you back. She had been born prematurely and complications resulted in her contracting double pneumonia twice in addition to scarlet fever. Later, a bout with polio left her leg crooked and her foot twisted inward. She spent most of her childhood in braces.

But Wilma had heart. At the age of six, while riding on a bus to a hospital in Nashville, forty-five miles south of her home town, she said to herself, "I'm going to travel out of this small town and make my place in the world."

Each time she went to the hospital for her checkup she asked the doctor, "When will I get to take these braces off and walk?"

"We'll see," the doctor kept saying.

"Honey, the most important thing in life is for you to believe and keep on trying," a loving, supportive mother reassured.

By age eleven, Wilma began sneaking around, taking off her braces, and slowly and painfully walking about the house for hours, getting one of her brothers or sisters to stand watch for her. Finally, she confessed to her doctor that she had been taking the braces off. She took them off in his office and demonstrated how she sometimes walked about her house. The doctor gave her permission to remove them sometimes. That was all the permission she needed—she never put them on again!

At age twelve she began traveling with her older sister's basketball team as a chaperone. The following year, she made the basketball and track teams. The first time Wilma ran a race, she found she could beat her closest friend. Then she beat all the other girls in her high school, and then every high school girl in the state.

Two years later, she tried out for the internationally known Tennessee State University "Tigerbelles," a summer program for high school students. She met Mae Faggs, a teammate who had made two U.S. Olympic teams in the past and who inspired Wilma to try out for the U.S. Olympic team that was scheduled to run in the 1956 Olympic Games in Australia.

At the Olympic Trials, held at American University in Washington, D.C., Wilma began by leading the pack in the 200-meter dash qualifying heats. Startled to find herself out in front, ahead of Mae Faggs, she looked around to see where the other runners were and Mae sped by to come in first. Wilma was second. "I'm disappointed in you," Mae scolded after the meet. "Qualifying isn't enough; you've always got to go for that gold."

Wilma reached the semi-finals of the 200-meter dash

at the 1956 Olympic Games in Melbourne but was finally eliminated. She did, however, win a bronze medal as a member of the team in the women's 400-meter relay. When her friends congratulated her, she was embarrassed because she knew that she had failed. She believed she had what it took to win a gold medal. She vowed that that kind of performance would never happen again. She was only sixteen, but she made a firm commitment to win in 1960.

When she enrolled in Tennessee State University, Wilma began her vigorous training for the upcoming Olympics. The agonizing reality of what it takes to become a world class runner would discourage most young women. But Wilma not only maintained her grueling training schedule, she also worked to pay her way through college and maintained the B average required to stay on the track team.

While most people would have been satisfied to "get by," Wilma had the heart to become a champion. She not only fulfilled all of the academic requirements, but also engaged in an exhausting do-it-yourself program on her own. She would sneak down the dormitory fire escape to run on the track from 8:00 to 10:00 P.M. Then she would climb back up the fire escape and into bed in time for bed checks. Day after day, for more than three years, she maintained the same monotonous and demanding schedule.

By 1960 she was ready. When Wilma walked out on the stadium field that summer in Rome, nearly eighty thousand fans cheered wildly, sensing she was to be one of those special Olympic champions who would capture the hearts of spectators around the world. In three electrifying performances she won three gold medals, becoming the first American woman to win three gold medals in track and field.

Wilma Rudolph—the little crippled girl who refused to buckle under pressure, the valiant teenager who had not given in to the comforts of life, the college coed who pushed herself beyond all normal human endurance—had become a living legend.

Much has happened to reward her for her discipline and sacrifices in the years since those magic moments in the stadium in Rome. She has been honored by ticker tape parades, White House receptions, numerous awards, a book and movie of her life, and countless interviews on television and in newspapers. Through it all she has kept the quiet dignity of a true high achiever.

In her book, *Wilma: The Story of Wilma Rudolph*, she writes, "When you're running, you're involved. You're always in the process of trying to master something. And you never quite get there. I guess that's what makes the so-called champion: the willingness to continue to work and strive to improve your excellence every day."

These days you'll find Wilma encouraging high school students, prospective Olympic stars, and people from all walks of life to rise above the circumstances they face and become the high achievers they were created to be. What she loves best is giving classes, seminars, and financial support through the Wilma Rudolph Foundation in Indianapolis, which helps underprivileged and handicapped people to achieve their goals.

It is foolish to attribute Wilma's marvelous achievements to good luck. Every person who has ever become a true high achiever recognizes that people like her become champions despite their circumstances, rather than because of them.

People Will Try To Hold You Back

As you set out to become a high achiever, there may be people who try to hold you back. Some of them will want you to settle for living safely and doing what is expected of you—in other words, to conform. Most of those who seek to hold you back sincerely care about you, but simply do not understand your high goals.

General George S. Patton, Jr. said about the determination you need to overcome the tug of people against you as you reach for high goals:

You have to be single minded,
Drive only for one thing on which you have decided.
And if it looks as if you might be getting there,
All kinds of people, including some you thought were
 your loyal friends,
Will suddenly show up . . .
 to trip you, blacken you,
And break your spirit.

Three years after my Matterhorn climb, I was making plans to climb Mount Kilimanjaro in Africa. My wife, aware that Kilimanjaro is a mile higher than the Matterhorn and consequently much more physically demanding, made a doctor's appointment for me to have a complete physical examination. "According to our tests and graphs," said the doctor, "you have ten percent more lung capacity than the average male your age, height, and weight. But," he added jokingly, "you seem to have *twenty percent fewer brains*!"

If you are to become a high achiever, face the fact that the higher and more unusual your goals, the more others will try to discourage you from them, even in jest.

You Are Your Greatest Obstacle

If your preoccupation in life is to remain comfortable and do what you're told, you will never become a high achiever. Virtually every great achievement of history was preceded by an individual's intense effort to accomplish a high goal, regardless of the loss of comfort or the opinion of others.

The so-called self-motivation experts often refer to Proverbs 23:7. Unfortunately, they tend to misquote it, and the difference is astounding. Their translation is usually this: "For as a man thinketh, so is he." What the proverb actually says is, "For as he thinketh *in his heart*, so is he. . . ."

There's nothing wrong with using your head, but it's your heart that makes the critical difference. Many people have great ideas, brilliant insights, and clever schemes, but they lack the heart to carry them out. Aristotle wisely said, "I count him braver who overcomes his desires than him who conquers his enemies; for the hardest victory is the victory over self."

Four Ways To Spell "Heart"

You can spell heart *courage.* Heart is the courage to do what the masses won't. The great enemy of courage is not cowardice, but conformity.

The vast majority of people yield to the pressures of conformity because it is safe. It is unconventional to set your sights high, to climb out of ruts. That takes courage.

Heart can also be spelled *persistence.* High achievement in life is not reserved only for the talented or those with high IQs. It is not a gift of birth. High achievement is dependent upon one's drive and persistence, on one's extra effort. High achievers know that their bodies and minds are always pushing for comfort and ease but that the road to high achievement is all uphill. A truly persistent person struggles against overwhelming obstacles, labors in the face of sharp criticism, and does what few if any understand. As the old saying goes: "A big shot is only a little shot who kept shooting."

You can also spell heart *perspective*. When you're climbing, the perspective is different from when you're in the valleys. People tend to focus their attention on the difficulties they encounter, the unpleasant things that arise, and the pains associated with struggling. But when you have heart you view things with broader perspective and see life more positively. You look for the good in situations, even when it's hard to find.

Finally, you can spell heart *purpose*. Ralph Waldo Emerson wrote in his essay "Circles," "Nothing great was ever achieved without enthusiasm." And true enthusiasm comes from giving ourselves to a purpose. High achievers have a purpose, and they have the heart to pursue it when other people quit.

How Do You Develop Heart?

Here is an exercise that will help you develop the heart of a high achiever. First, take out a plain sheet of paper and write at the top one of your highest goals. Next, divide the remainder of the paper into two equal sides by making a straight line down the middle. Label the left side "Why?" and label the right side "Why Not?" Start with the "Why?" side and list every possible reason why you should pursue this goal. When you finish, switch to the "Why Not?" side and list every reason why you should not pursue this goal. Now count separately the number of reasons you list on each side. If you have actually picked a high goal, then your "Why Not?" reasons are certain to outnumber your "Why?" reasons by as many as four to one. Most people would now conclude that the logical decision would be to give up this goal. The high achiever, on the other hand, would never be deterred by lists and numbers and would persist despite the odds.

As you climb closer to that goal, be forewarned that you will want to quit. This is natural and happens to all high achievers. But remember that quitting and wanting to quit are two entirely different things. Ever since I started working toward high goals, I have thought of many reasons to quit. However, my "heart" has always kept me from quitting—my will to become a high achiever has never failed me.

PART THREE

High Achievement—Putting It into Action

You can read motivational books, listen to inspirational tapes, observe remarkable people, and acquire all six of the attitudes I discussed in the last section. However, unless you *act,* your efforts will do you no good.

This section addresses the action phase of high achievement. First, I'm going to share with you the three *peak principles* that will help you along your way. You are familiar with the *attitudes* of high achievers, but you'll also need this *concrete advice.*

1. Always climb fully equipped.
2. Set progressively higher intermediate climbing goals.
3. Count on goal-climbing momentum.

Secondly, I'm going to discuss the dynamics of high goal setting and achievement. How do we know when we've achieved success? How can we continue to be successful? Anyone can accomplish one or two great things in his life, but that doesn't make him successful forever. Any great accomplishment is subject to atrophy. We either continue developing or we deteriorate.

Let's take a look at success in terms of dynamics:

1. Success is the progressive realization of worthy goals or ideals. In other words, the moment you *decide* on a goal and *begin* working toward it, you are successful.
2. Success is the progressive realization of becoming the person God created you to be.

According to those two definitions, high achievement is a dynamic process by which your ongoing actions produce the results you desire.

The dynamics of high achivement consist of the following guidelines that I will discuss in separate chapters: living by the rules of summitry, choosing accurate goals, using your personal High Goal Climbing Planner and following the High Goals Cycle, and seeing life as a series of renewals.

10

The Three Peak Principles of High Achievement

Peak Principle #1: Always Climb Fully Equipped

As I traveled around the world, climbing some of its great mountains, I always had a choice of climbing in one of two ways: I could either climb fully equipped or I could climb the hard way. Without exception I chose to climb fully equipped, which meant that I hired one or more expert guides, an outfitter, and bearers.

Expert Guides

The Matterhorn is not a mountain to be taken casually. Climbers of all ages and nationalities have died of exposure, from fatigue, or by falling. High and ferocious winds, treacherous ledges, melting snow and ice that dislodge rocks, bone-chilling cold, and unpredictable weather pose grave dangers for the uninitiated climber. Knowing where, when, and how to climb is essential for the success and safety of anyone wanting to reach the top and climb back down again. That kind of knowledge comes only from an expert guide.

An expert guide is one who combines the wisdom of experience, the collective knowledge of the pioneers who have succeeded and failed, and the ability to assess the capabilities and limitations of the person being guided. The expert guide also knows how to communicate what must be done to reach the high goal, and to spot and correct mistakes before they become critical. He inspires confidence.

For me, Alfons Franzen had all those qualities. I knew he was the kind of guide I could trust with my life. I knew there would be times he would give instructions that would seem illogical; that he would make demands difficult to fulfill; and that if necessary, he would rebuke me for my errors in judgment.

I had hoped that as we climbed together I would come to like him as a person. However, liking him was not nearly as important as respecting and trusting him. I needed to have absolute confidence in his abilities and to obey his instructions.

In that long climb there were times I questioned him. When I was blowing on my frostbitten hands, attempting to thaw them, his command to "beat 'em on the rocks" went against everything I felt. Yet when I obeyed his stern orders, I found that he was right.

I'll never forget how I felt when he told me to go first on our climb down. He tied the belay rope around me, winding a couple of extra loops around my waist. With a twinkle in his eyes he said, "It'll be more comfortable for you when you fall." Not "*if* you fall," but "*when* you fall."

Alfons was neither the first nor the last expert guide to help me reach a high goal. I've learned to rely on expert guides in every area of my life. In business, there have been a handful of expert guides who have saved me from costly mistakes, shown me how to take advantage of great opportunities, and kept me going when everything within me wanted to quit. My wife and our two children have been excellent guides as they've helped me discover how to work toward and enjoy a strong family relationship. Most important, I've learned to climb with expert guides in my spiritual life. Shortly after I returned from climbing the Matterhorn, I decided to turn my life over completely to the most expert guide in the universe—Jesus Christ. I've found Him to be the most reliable "Guide of guides" that anyone could ever follow. When you're dangling on a twisting, swirling rope a mile above a glacier floor where many skilled mountaineers have met their deaths, you know that *absolute confidence* is crucial to your survival. Absolute confidence goes far beyond the limits of mere self-confidence. I've found I can develop absolute confidence by trusting completely in Christ's guidance.

Expert guides can be found in a wide variety of places. They come in all shapes, sizes, and colors. You'll find excellent guides in books. For example, when I started preparing to run marathons, I found the writings of experienced marathon runners very helpful. They showed me how to train, how to conserve my energy, how to make every movement count, and how to pace myself.

People who have already been where you want to go make excellent guides. When I want business guidance,

I look for a person who has achieved success in business. I don't want to read the theories of someone who doesn't have firsthand experience.

The instructors in the mountain-climbing schools in Wyoming and Colorado taught me about the technical aspects of mountaineering. The biographies of great people taught me to lift my sights, and countless people in all walks of life have guided me through moments of confusion. Expert guides can always be found; however, you have to go looking for them—they won't come looking for you. The very best guides are often busy with their own high goals. While most of them are more than happy to offer you guidance, they won't seek you out.

Sometimes expert guides charge a fee for their advice. If professional guidance makes the difference between success and failure, the fee is a good investment. In any event, you must carefully choose the person who will lead you, observe him, and do precisely what he tells you to do every step of the way.

Choosing Outfitters and Bearers

Whenever I climb, I select an outfitter to supply my food, cooking gear, sleeping bag, and equipment. The outfitter I choose must have a great deal of experience in rigging climbers and must be able to provide for them. Remember, a high goal is one that you can only reach with help from other people, and I have discovered that it is a foolish waste of energy to do everything myself. One reason many achievers never become high achievers is that they try to carry all their own burdens. By hiring bearers to carry the burdens, I become free to climb higher than I could ever climb by myself.

Pulling It All Together

Most accidents in mountain climbing occur when climbers try to scale mountains the hard way without expert guidance. I have learned that only by climbing fully equipped in all areas of my life will I climb higher, make a larger contribution, and provide more valuable service to God and mankind.

How does one climb fully equipped in life? God has given each of us three dimensions to develop as we go through life: physical, mental, and spiritual. When these three dimensions combine, they compose a powerful whole. The individual parts are so interrelated that anything you can do to improve one improves the others. Likewise, anything you do that is harmful to one harms the others. To climb fully equipped to the heights of your potential, you simply have to use all of the resources you have been given. High achievment cannot be denied to the person who gives life everything—physically, mentally, and spiritually—and who always climbs fully equipped.

In the Yukon there is a saying about the dog sleds that supply the Eskimo villages: "The speed of the leader is the speed of the pack." That is, the pack of dogs pulling the sled will never be any faster than the speed of the lead dog. How true this is in all forms of leadership!

Our spiritual dimension is our leading dimension—God intended it that way. The speed of our spiritual dimension will determine how high and for how long a high achiever will climb in life. Your spiritual dimension demands at least as much attention as your physical and mental dimensions. The spiritual dimension needs to be fed and exercised or it grows weak and ineffective.

The most powerful motivational force that can stimulate high achievers is the belief that God is with them and inside them in the person of His son, Jesus Christ, and in the power of the Holy Spirit. The true high achiever must have this power, this confidence, and this capacity to climb fully equipped physically, mentally, and spiritually. A partially equipped person— no matter what natural talents he or she may have—is robbed of the dynamic power and ability to develop spiritually. Are you climbing fully equipped or are you settling for less?

Peak Principle #2: Set Progressively Higher Intermediate Climbing Goals

One reason so many would-be high achievers fail to reach their highest goals is that they shoot for the moon in a single shot. It is one thing to hold a lofty dream deep inside. It is quite another to commit yourself to fulfilling that dream immediately. High achievers have learned that they must break their lofty dreams into bite-sized intermediate goals: goals they can reach by expending great energy, but goals they *can* reach.

The salesperson who says after a motivational seminar, I'm going to double my sales during the next year! might be setting an unrealistic goal. The result is likely to be failure and discouragement. A more productive approach would be to decide what increase in sales calls for the next month would be possible and then set that as an intermediate goal. Once that is achieved, then set a higher goal.

Going for a high goal requires more confidence than any of us has when we begin to prepare for achievement. Confidence must be carefully put into place before we can realistically reach for the dream we have nourished. When I hung that picture of the Matterhorn on the wall of my den, I realized that I was far from ready to commit myself to the strenuous climb.

Intermediate Goals Get You Going

After I looked into my father's face that day in the intensive care unit at the hospital and decided I was going to do something to change my sedentary lifestyle, it was seven years before I began to work at changing my physical condition. The change began that day I resolved to set my first intermediate goal: running around the block which surrounded my house.

When I look back on that first intermediate goal, it seems small and insignificant. Yet it was a beginning because it gave me something tangible to do immediately. I knew I couldn't climb the Matterhorn, or even run a marathon, but I could build up to running that eight-tenths of a mile. Once I'd achieved that—and not one minute before—I was in a position to move on to bigger and better things.

Few of us ever make life-changing decisions. More often, we make a series of little decisions that set a course toward life-changing patterns. By the time we are

ready to make the big decisions, the options have been
narrowed by our little choices along the way. If we do
not focus our goals, our lives will be controlled by
haphazard decisions. Intermediate goals enable us to
make definite decisions toward the high goals of our
lives. They provide something tangible that will help us
reach our highest goal.

Peak Principle #3:
Count on Goal-Climbing Momentum

Probably the most common hindrance to becoming a
high achiever is the constant temptation to rest on past
achievements. All of us yearn for a place to rest comfor-
tably. However, if we pause too long after reaching an
intermediate goal, it can lower us to the ranks of the
nonachiever.

One of the possible hazards of high-altitude climbing
is freezing to death from the extremely cold temperatures. The most natural tendency of a person nearing
death from exposure is to look for a place to lie down
and sleep. Yet to lie down when you are nearly frozen is
to sign your own death warrant. All the expert guides
I've ever talked to on the subject say the same thing:
Keep moving! Whatever there is within you that screams
out for a long rest, to give in is to surrender to defeat.

In running the Terre Haute Marathon, every time I
passed a mileage marker—every time I achieved an intermediate goal—I was tempted to stop and rest. Yet I
knew that to do so would keep me from reaching my
high goal of running all the way.

Momentum Saves Energy

Nothing can preserve your creative energy and stamina like momentum. It's as simple as the law of inertia, which says: "A body at rest tends to remain at rest, and a body in motion tends to remain in motion—at the same speed and in the same direction—unless acted upon by an outside force." Remember, it takes less energy to keep on climbing than it does to hang on a ledge!

Coaches, athletes, and sportscasters talk about momentum all the time. In a crucial football game, the offensive team makes a critical score and the momentum swings in their direction. When the defense takes the field, they usually play with an intensity that has not been present before. The team that can take advantage of momentum usually wins.

An airliner's engines must be set at full throttle to get up enough speed to overcome the drag and gravity that hold it back on take-off. Once the plane becomes airborne, the pilot pulls back on the throttles to save fuel. Even though the engines are getting less fuel, they continue to push the airliner faster and faster. Why? Momentum!

Goal-climbing momentum works in exactly the same way. Those people who learn how to take advantage of the momentum they gain by achieving become the high achievers. They always seem to have greater enthusiasm, more energy, and more stamina than other people.

There are many forces at work to hold you back as you seek to become a high achiever. If you want to reach high goals, always remember to count on goal-climbing momentum.

Exhilaration is a Great Motivator

There is another feeling that accompanies the accomplishment of an intermediate goal—exhilaration. The person who is exhilarated receives a new burst of energy that can enable him or her to keep moving despite the overpowering urge to stop and rest.

I'm not saying that you shouldn't enjoy your victories. Celebrating is good for the morale, pausing to express gratitude for the help you've received in making the goal is a must, and enjoying the fruits of your labors keeps you happy. However, it is crucial that you set your next intermediate goal while you're feeling exhilarated from attaining the goal you've just reached. That way, you take advantage of the joy of achievement, the excitement of seeing a dream come true, and the enthusiasm and confidence you feel when you know you've done something difficult, without being tempted to rest on your laurels.

11

Living by the Rules
of Summitry

Have you ever wondered why people climb mountains? After all, it seems so useless to the average person. Why risk your life? Why expose yourself to unbelievable cold and discomfort? Why spend a lot of money and go against the better advice of your friends and family just to climb to the top of a mountain, when all you do after you get there is climb back down? Maybe the fascination with mountain climbing has to do with asserting one's mastery over life, proving that there is no challenge too great. Perhaps it is simply to experience the ultimate that nature has to offer, to be surrounded by the sensation of the world at your feet, to view the fertile valleys and barren peaks shimmering with ice with only heaven above you.

As a confirmed mountain climber, let me ask you why you have *not* climbed the world's great mountains. I'm not suggesting that you climb actual mountains, but why aren't you climbing to the highest level of your potential right now? What's holding you back?

What Is Summitry?

Summitry is a word I have coined to describe the continuous achievement of becoming the person God created you to be. It is not what you have done but what you are becoming. Are you satisfied with the person you have become or are becoming? What type of person are you really? Forget all your accomplishments and achievements. What are you like inside? Do you like what you see? Are others attracted to you for what you have done or own, or for what you have become as a person?

Your performance as a high achiever should not be limited to one or two categories of life. You have responsibilities to God, spouse, family, career, health, finances, recreation, community and nation, and fellow man.

The rules of summitry dictate that you maintain a *balance* of activities and interests, divided among all of the areas of your responsibility. The individual who devotes his or her time to a career, at the expense of family relationships, God, health, or anything else, cannot be called a success. Remember, no matter how successful you are in one area, you will only be as successful as your lowest achievement in any of your areas of responsibility. Jesus said: "For what does it profit a man if he should gain the whole world and lose his own soul?"

High achievers climb to great heights in their personal lives, in their careers, with their families, and in their spiritual lives in order to discover precious things about themselves. It's always difficult for the high achiever to settle for the ordinary, the dull, or the passive in any area of responsibility.

To realize your potential within all areas of responsibility, you must set goals for each one. That way, there are no weak links in your life, no regrets, only the synergistic effect of all of the parts fitting together into a powerful and wonderful whole.

Now I want to turn to the three rules of summitry for the high achiever: (1) the power of purpose, (2) climbing from peak to peak, and (3) smelling the flowers along the way.

The Power of Purpose

I will never forget what my parents said to me when I announced that I was going to start mountain climbing. I had explained that I would like to climb not so much to stand on the peak but to learn things about myself through the preparation and the struggling—things that I could learn in no other way.

"Fine," they said, "then go through with the preparation, but don't make the final climb." My first thought was How absurd! But as I thought about it more, the statement seemed logical. If the meaning is in the preparation, why go to the top?

I later realized that going to the top is what gives the preparation meaning. As an achiever or even a high achiever, you may succeed beyond your wildest dreams, but you will never succeed beyond the purpose to which you dedicate your life. The height of your accomplishments will never be any greater than the purpose to which they are attached.

A major problem facing many people today is a lack of meaning and purpose in their lives. Joy eludes them, cynicism and distrust abound, and uneasiness underlies their consumption of pleasures. They lack a purpose in life. They ask, Why do this? What should I do? Why am I here? Where did I come from? Where am I going? They are looking for something to grab onto, something that makes sense—not shallow ideals but those with substance. They are looking for a real purpose that will give their lives meaning.

Purpose is the engine, the power that drives and directs our lives. Purpose is our contribution to life—that overpowering reason that enables us to answer the question, "What am I living for?"

What's Your Purpose in Life?

It was never my purpose in life to become a mountain climber. While I have great admiration for those who are lured to conquer mountains again and again, that would be an empty lifestyle for me. My purpose in life is to become all God created me to be. Climbing mountains has only been a series of stepping stones along that pathway. I chose mountaineering, running marathons, and building a business as intermediate goals because they held high interest for me. I knew that whatever I chose as a way of achieving my purpose in life would have to be interesting and fun enough to keep me motivated.

There are many purposes available to you, and it is absolutely essential to know what you believe is most important in life. You should be able to put into a few words your purpose for living. It is only then that you can choose intermediate and high goals from all the options available.

What's your purpose in life? One way to discover it is to write your own mock-obituary. Sit down and write what you would like to be remembered for. Once you realize what you want to do with your life, it's amazing how clear the steps you should take become. As long as you muddle through life with no direction, you will always be confused about your next move.

Reading the biographies of great people, I've noticed that each person had a purpose. Harrison Kinney wrote in *The Last Supper of Leonardo da Vinci:*

> It was as though Leonardo regarded his masterpiece throughout its creation as a partial payment to God for the divine gift of mortal genius. For Leonardo knew well that no man is ordained to possess universal insight to hoard the knowledge; a man who catches fire from the sparks of a cosmic awareness must kindle other fires or be consumed himself. The *Last Supper* was Leonardo's spiritual acknowledgment of indebtedness. There could be no postponement of labor where it was concerned; no bickering over the material terms of payment.

In other words, one can interpret that da Vinci's purpose in life was to attempt to repay his indebtedness to God for the gift of genius he had received. His high goal was to create a work of art that would express this feeling and move people to an awareness of God. It is doubtful that he could have foreseen how many millions of lives his masterpiece would profoundly affect in the centuries to follow.

High achievers are caught up in a purpose that is bigger than themselves, often exceeding even their highest goals. Many of them leave marks in history that can only be fully appreciated in later centuries.

Purpose vs. Goal

How is a purpose different from a goal? A purpose is an underlying commitment that shapes a person's actions, directions, and attitudes about life. It is well understood but not necessarily measurable. To be a good father is a purpose. To give glory to God is a purpose. Sometimes, purposes run deep enough that we are willing to give our lives for them. They answer the question, Why?

A goal, on the other hand, is more measurable, more specific, more confined to a time span. Goals best answer the question, What? They are the specific ways we express the underlying purpose of our lives, the actions we take because of the purposes that guide us. To climb the Matterhorn is a goal. To read one book per week is a goal. To spend thirty minutes in prayer and meditation each day is a goal.

The best way to determine what your purposes are is to take a look at the goals that are guiding your actions. Goals are the tools which make solid purposes become realities. Your mind, your body, and your spiritual being needs specific instructions. If your purposes are unselfish, then you will be unselfish in the goals you set; if they are honest, your goals will be honest. Your future will not depend on economic conditions, outside influences, or circumstances over which you have no control, but on your purposes in life and on linking your goals to those purposes.

Without a high purpose in life, occasional accomplishments will mislead a person, and often those around him. A high purpose enables us to move to higher levels of achievement without the self-destructiveness of blind ambition. It can set us free from the thirst for power and control over others. We can begin to tackle greater feats without the overpowering dread that our actions will become more important to us than our personal existence.

The truly great person is the one who has been tested and found trustworthy, is motivated from within, and has yielded to a high purpose. That person is ready for the big job, ready to climb to higher and higher peaks.

Climbing from Peak to Peak

Many achievers never become high achievers because they do not acquire the habit of climbing from peak to peak. Certainly, a nagging itch may be satisfied by recognition from peers, but too much limelight can also breed contentment and make it harder for the achiever to "back down" to the risk and hardship of higher achievement. The greatness of the big achievement is a transitory experience.

If you are standing on the peak of a mountain and want to reach a higher peak, you cannot go in a straight line from one peak to another. Why? Because there is no ground there to support you. The same is true in any area of human achievement. In order to get from one peak to another, you must go down before you can go back up. You must be willing to climb back down from the high energy level of your last accomplishment into the valley of risk, hardship, and preparation before you can climb to a new achievement.

The best way to de-energize and then re-energize yourself is to celebrate your victory. You celebrate by combining reward with recommitment. Reward yourself in some special way. Take others along with you—your family, friends, or associates. Let them be a part of the fun, the de-energizing process. Let them also be a part of your commitment to your next goal. But don't dwell too long on the victory—you'll lose momentum!

Once you start climbing to a new goal, the best advice I can give you is to keep climbing until you get there. It is not important how long it takes to reach a high goal; what is important is that you reach it. Very few people ever ask me, How long did it take you to run the marathon? or, How long did it take you to climb the Matterhorn?

An article by Peter Boardman in *Mountain Magazine* quotes Friedrich Nietzsche: "There are two tragedies in a man's life. One is not having reached one's goal, and the second is having reached it. The second is the greater." What is left unsaid here is that attaching goals to a purpose in life greater than both the goal and the self eliminates the futility and self-destructive tragedy of having reached a goal.

When your focus is on what you are becoming, rather than on what you are accomplishing, you are willing to pay the price of starting the long climb to another, higher peak. If the reverse is true, you can only see the trip down and up again as losing ground.

Many people continue to work at jobs they hate because they define success in terms of their salaries, their fringe benefits, and their titles. For them, it is unthinkable to drop back to a lower income—or no income—in order to start an upward climb toward independence and self-determination. You cannot climb from one peak to another as long as you are hanging onto the pinnacle you have reached. You must be willing to redefine success if that is what it takes to climb to another peak.

The Real Joy in Climbing

The moment of greatest joy for a high achiever comes when "the light is spotted at the end of the tunnel." It comes at that instant when you recognize that *you are going to make it*! It's that marvelous moment when you realize, way down inside, that you have been right, that you do have what it takes, that you really are going to reach your high goal.

In fact, reaching the high goal is usually anticlimactic. It's almost as if you feel let down; the excitement is not as great as you expected. The real joy of high achievement comes in the struggle, not in the victory.

At the moment of victory, the high achiever is flooded with a realization that his accomplishment will help him become a greater person. He knows that this achievement will set in motion actions toward higher goals and possibilities. His thoughts turn immediately to the next peak.

Smell the Flowers Along the Way

One of the most common errors high achievers make is to concentrate on the future to the extent that the present loses its meaning. Consequently, they miss important opportunities to enjoy the journey along the path they travel.

Some years ago, when I left my job in a large corporation to be a small business entrepreneur, I met an elderly gentleman who had successfully built his own company. He told me I would be working harder than I'd ever worked before and that I would never really be able to "leave my work at the office" again; these sacrifices were just part of the life of an entrepreneur. Then he added, "Be sure to smell the flowers along the way!" I have never forgotten his advice.

There is more to achievement than keeping score, more to life than work, and more to work than just the attainment of goals. The most satisfied high achievers are those who concentrate on each day as it comes. They are aware of their surroundings and appreciate the friends, the associates, and the little joys along the way. They have the least difficulty leading a full life in their later years.

Life is meant for accomplishments, but it is also meant for enjoyment and fond memories with those special people around you. Defeat, pain, tragedy, and sorrow will come to each of us. However, we can face them all with courage and dignity if we have taken the time to "stop and smell the flowers along the way."

I know it's hard to stop and savor life when the struggle is great, the time seems short, and the challenge requires every ounce of your concentration. However, taking time to enjoy the present moment can often make the difference between success and failure—even between life and death.

When I was climbing Mount Kilimanjaro the thin air at the extremely high altitude made it very hard to breathe. I found myself gasping for air like a person with a serious lung disease. Then I began to taste, smell, and savor the air, and I became aware that there was more air than I had thought.

Savor the bittersweet taste of struggle. Smell the aroma of friendship. Take time off, spend time with your family, go on vacations, have evenings out with your spouse, do something different—your high achievement will wait. In fact, if you take time out to enjoy living, you will be better equipped to reach your high goal.

There you have them, the three rules of summitry: (1) let purpose put the power into your life, (2) be willing to climb from peak to peak, and, (3) smell the flowers along the way.

If you will live your life of high achievement by those rules of summitry, you will discover that they contain the sustenance to keep you going when everything within you wants to quit and when all the circumstances of life seem to imprison you. Remember, high achievement is not what you accomplish, but what you are becoming.

12

Accuracy in Choosing Goals

Today, we think of Albert Schweitzer as a hero. We think of his work, which won him the 1952 Nobel Peace Prize, as being achievement of the finest order. However, to his friends and associates in 1905, his announcement that he was going to pursue a life-long dream seemed almost insane.

Schweitzer, a world-renown theologian, teacher, author, and musician, announced that he was going to become a doctor and go to Africa as a medical missionary. His colleagues in several European countries tried desperately to dissuade him from wasting his talents. To them, his resources would be wasted on the "savages" of Africa.

No one could convince Schweitzer that his high goal was unrealistic or unworthy of his talents. He resigned his university appointment in 1906 and entered medical school. In 1913, having completed his medical studies, he went to Africa and devoted the remainder of his life to treating the diseased and poverty-ridden Gabonese people.

Without backing from any organization, he almost single-handedly built his own hospital, often laboring way into the night with only slight help from the people of the little village of Lambarene in Gabon. However, fifty years later when he received his "address of felicitation" from his supporters in 28 countries, there were about 350 patients in his hospital and more than 150 patients in his leper colony nearby.

Was Albert Schweitzer's choice of goals accurate for him? It appears so. In response to those who questioned how he had chosen to live his life he once said, "Every start upon an untrodden path is a venture, which, only in unusual circumstances, looks sensible and likely to be successful."

Life is a process of making decisions, of selecting our daily activities. Ultimately, each of us must decide alone which road he will choose.

Choosing Goals Appropriate to You

How can we know what goals are appropriate for us? How can we be sure that the goals we choose suit our abilities, our interests, our overall purpose in life?

Goals are very personal. A realistic goal for one person is not necessarily a realistic goal for another. It may be entirely realistic for a budding young athlete to dream about becoming a gold medal runner in the Olympics. However, it is not realistic for a youngster who has lost both legs to set that goal.

Likewise, a goal which is appropriate for one point in our lives may not be at all realistic at another point. It may be fine for a sixteen-year-old to set a goal of becoming an astronaut but unrealistic for a fifty-five-year-old.

What goals are realistic for you now? What goals are reachable? Would the following high goals be appropriate, realistic, and reachable for you?

1. Winning the world championship in boxing
2. Playing professional basketball
3. Making a million dollars during the next year
4. Writing a best-selling book
5. Becoming president of a Fortune 500 company

For most of you, these high goals are probably unrealistic. To some of you, one or more of them might qualify as appropriate.

But what about these goals?

1. Learning a new language
2. Doubling your income during the next five years
3. Becoming a certified scuba diver
4. Going to Africa as a missionary
5. Starting your own company

A greater number of you probably felt that the second set of goals was more appropriate for you than the first.

Four Questions To Help You Accurately Choose Goals

In Proverbs 12:11, the Bible says, "He who works his land will have abundant food, but he who chases fantasies lacks judgment." How do you know what is an appropriate goal and what is just a fantasy? Here are four questions that might help you make that decision.

1.   Is the proposed goal consistent with the way you see yourself? In our last chapter we talked about the importance of having a life that is powered by purpose. When you consider a goal, it is best to focus on your underlying purpose for life and to ask if the goal is consistent with your purpose. Will it lead you toward fulfilling your purpose? Are there other goals you could direct your energies toward that would lead you more quickly to fulfilling your purpose?

Zig Ziglar says, "You cannot consistently perform in a manner that is inconsistent with the way you see yourself." Goals that lead you away from your purpose in life are never appropriate choices.

2.   Is your goal worthy of your very best efforts? It is better to shoot at a high goal and miss than it is to aim for a low goal and hit it. Many people who are widely acclaimed as successful are really failures because they could have done so much more with their lives.

Is the goal you are considering high enough for you to approach enthusiastically and earnestly—to give it the best you have? If the answer to that question is no, then the goal you are considering is not an accurate choice for you. If you can truthfully say to yourself that the goal you are considering is worthy of your very best efforts, then it could be an appropriate goal for you.

It is often said that people work themselves to death, but I doubt that statement is true. It is much more likely that these people actually die from the tension, stress, and emotional fatigue that come from pursuing unworthy or inappropriate goals.

3.   Is your goal consistent with the way God sees you? You were created in the image of God, and your goals should reflect that image. When God created you,

He had a high purpose in mind for you and endowed you with the capabilities for reaching high goals. Also, He provided you with tremendous resources for accomplishing these goals. If you settle for something less than you were created to be, you act in a manner inconsistent with the way God sees you.

4. Is your goal consistent with your values? When considering a goal, you must think of how that goal will affect all your responsibilities. For example, if you are considering a career goal that will consume tremendous amounts of time and energy, what will that do to your family goals? To your community goals? To your spiritual development?

That's why it's crucial that you keep the values of your life in clear focus. One of the most common mistakes people make when choosing a goal is to value things and use people. The exact opposite is true for the high achiever. The high achiever, in every area of responsibility, always values people and uses things. When you are convinced that a goal is in keeping with your values, then you have made a wise choice.

Appropriate Intermediate Goals— Stepping-Stones to Your High Goal

In the beginning, high goals can seem so far away that they are hard to see as real possibilities. When I was struggling to run mini-marathons, my picture of the Matterhorn seemed vague and unreal. Would I ever be physically, mentally, and spiritually prepared to take on the challenge of climbing it? But like all high achievers, I set about to accomplish intermediate goals along the way to that lofty peak.

If you have high goals, what are you doing today to lead yourself toward them? Have you set an appropriate series of progressively higher intermediate goals that will take you ever closer to your high goals? If not, you are likely to spend your life with dreamers who long to do great things but are not willing to take the steps necessary to achieve them.

Appropriate intermediate goals are stepping-stones to high achievement. If your high goal is to become a skilled brain surgeon, and you are still an undergraduate, are you striving to make good enough grades to get into medical school? If your high goal is to become an astronaut and pilot a space shuttle to the moon, are you now developing the kind of physical stamina and mental alertness that will lead you to that goal?

In my seminars I often meet people who have very high goals but no appropriate intermediate goals. They want to achieve great things but they are not leading themselves toward their goals.

It's this simple: If you want to become a successful salesperson, you must make the daily calls necessary for making sales. Most successful salespeople have learned that it takes a lot more than simply having a good product to be successful. They know it requires working long hours, carefully planning everything they do, and preparing themselves to be the best salesperson they can possibly be. Then, with a good product, they can become successful.

Make sure you set a timetable for the completion of each intermediate goal. A desire is only a fantasy until you lock it down with a specific time commitment. Then it becomes an intermediate goal.

One word of caution: Don't engrave your intermediate goals, and the dates for completing them, in stone. You might be able to accelerate the accomplishment of your intermediate goals, and should not be satisfied to pause too long to rest between them. Likewise, you may discover that you have not allowed enough time for the completion of some of your intermediate goals. It is always wise to plan as carefully as possible, but also to remain flexible enough so that you can adjust to changing conditions, opportunities, and circumstances.

The great benefit of setting and achieving appropriate intermediate goals is that the moment you begin working on them, you become a high achiever. You don't have to wait until you have climbed to the top of a mountain to call yourself a mountaineer. All it takes is an active involvement in the pursuit of your high goal. Remember, high achievement is not what you do but what you become.

At least once a month the nation's newspapers carry a story of some famous person who has fallen onto hard times—tragic stories of great celebrities, athletes, or successful business people who have become alcoholics or drug addicts, who have lost everything they once had. Whether you have succeeded beyond your dreams or failed beyond your worst fears matters little. What matters is what you are doing now to become or remain a high achiever.

Life is a constant process of choosing which goals to pursue. If we choose our goals accurately then we can be high achievers and enjoy becoming the person God created us to be. We can stretch our minds, our bodies, and our spirits to their full potential as creatures made in the image of God.

13

Using Your High-Achievement Tools

In this book you have had the chance to share my joy in high achievement. If you have been moved to seek it on your own, then this book will have served its purpose.

Every endeavor in life requires certain tools. The two tools every high achiever will want to master are the High Goal Climbing Planner and the High Goals Cycle. These will help you to organize and maintain your high goal climbing momentum.

Remember to start slowly, develop respect for your high goals, and learn your limits. Then you can stretch as you climb. Above all else, enjoy the climb. Or, as Grove Patterson, the late editor-in-chief of the *Toledo Daily Blade*, stated it: "We came from someplace and we're going someplace . . . so we should make our time here an exciting adventure."

Setting Your Own High Goals

The first step in developing your personal High Goal Climbing Planner is to pick a goal in one of your nine areas of responsibility (see page 126). Maybe you have chosen a high goal for your business, or for your family, or in your community life. Whatever you choose, be sure it is a high goal. Remember, a high goal is one you cannot reach on your own: you must have help from other people to achieve it.

Once you've picked your high goal, write it down. By writing down your high goal with the sincere intent to achieve it, you are setting in motion a chain of events that will one day make it real.

Next, lock yourself in: Commit yourself to the task of accomplishing your high goal. To strengthen that commitment, tell others about your high goal. It doesn't matter if they think you are crazy. What matters is that you have made the commitment.

Guidelines

For each of the nine responsibility areas, here are some thoughts and guidelines that will help you set specific goals.

1. God. Our most important responsibility in life is our individual relationship with God. This is not a matter of religion, but of a relationship. Many people know about God, but don't know Him personally as a warm, loving, and just God. The first goal the high achiever should set is to develop a personal relationship with God. I have met many people who are highly intelligent in various fields but who have never taken a serious and honest look at Jesus Christ. God is revealed to us through our personal experience with Jesus Christ; otherwise we can never really know God.

The next goal should revolve around the exciting adventure of discovering God's purpose for your life. He has put each of us here for a purpose, and it's our responsibility to discover it. Only by learning more about God and how He works can we unravel and experience God's plan—his love, power, and purpose for our life. Expect big things from God, and you will receive them.

2. Spouse. Your spouse is a separate and distinct area of responsibility. He or she is not to be lumped into the next area of responsibility, the family, as is so often the case.

A partnership in business demands that both partners give a little extra to each other even after many other employees have joined the company. It is the same way with marriage. Your goals in this area should include having a dialogue with your spouse every day. If you're out of town, call him or her. Arrange a quiet dinner perhaps once a week. Maintain a "dating" relationship throughout your marriage. Seek to discover areas of your spouse's life to which you can contribute. And finally, set your high goals together.

3. Family. Caution: This area may be your toughest challenge. How often do we hear about some successful person whose personal family life is in shambles? Don't let this happen. Beware, as family problems start slowly and can get away from you before you know it.

Each high achiever needs to be overly sensitive in setting goals for his or her family. Budget one hour per day to spend with your children no matter what their ages. You may start by sitting down with them on the floor, then progress to playing with toys and games, to making crafts, and to reading books together. You may need to get into better physical condition to be a full participant with your kids in sports and on adventurous trips. You may even want to climb mountains together.

As a high achiever, make your family a part of your high achievements. Look for ways to involve them, such as taking one of your children with you on a business trip. Be an example, not an intimidator. And finally, be sure you share with them the love of God.

4.   Career. High achievers tend to give most of their time and effort to their careers, sometimes to the detriment of other responsibilities.

As you set high goals, determine your strengths and weaknesses and how you can contribute positively to the lives of other people in your work environment. Where your heart is, there your treasure will be.

5.   Health.

We are what we eat! said the wise old man,
And Lord if that's true, then I'm a garbage can.
   —from "The Fat Man's Prayer" by Victor Buono

The high achiever needs to be physically fit. Not only do physically fit people eat properly, but they manage time more wisely, get the sleep they need, recognize stress symptoms more readily, and are more confident and effective in their personal relationships.

Our body is a temple and we have the responsibility to maintain it wisely. Fitness seems to preserve the mental attitude of youth. Reassess your diet and see if what you are eating and drinking is healthy for you. Commit one hour of time every other day to vigorous physical exercise so that you have a healthy and energetic life. Start exercising slowly, but continue it as a habit. You'll begin to enjoy not only the exercise itself, but also the private time it gives you to think and reflect.

6. Finances. Thanks to challenging careers, many high achievers—although of course not all—are well blessed in this category. However, the fiscal resources with which God endows us are only loaned to us for the time being, and we have to be good stewards.

As a high achiever, adopt the habit of tithing. It's rewarding to be able to give graciously to others in need: to the church and other worthy causes. The gift of giving should be the product of the gift of earning.

7. Recreation. True recreation, like true rest, leaves the high achiever with greater energy and awareness. Recreation of your mind, body, and spirit should be stimulating, not desensitizing. Unfortunately, many people view recreation merely as a time for lethargy. They indulge themselves with excessive inactivity that leaves them clouded and sapped of energy.

Select an activity or sport for your recreation that you enjoyed as a child or would like to have enjoyed as a child. Chances are it will probably appeal to you now. At least once in your life you should experience a great recreational adventure, an adventure as thrilling as mountain climbing. Never again will you settle for the common, the ordinary, the dull, or the passive. The kind of recreation you choose helps determine the kind of person you become.

8. Community and nation. Chances are neither you nor I could have reached the heights we've reached—or plan to reach—had we lived under a more restrictive government and economic system.

Every high achiever in this country has a responsibility to defend and support his community and nation and what they stand for: democracy and the free enterprise system. As a high achiever your views and participation will be valued more highly than others. Opportunities will be made available for you to speak and to serve.

Seize them! Our country, government, and economic system helped make you what you are.

9.   *Fellow man.* We are indeed our brother's keeper. I suggest you try this exercise.

> Make a list of all the wonderful contributions to your life that were made by other people. Then make another list of all the wonderful contributions that you have made to other human beings. Which is the longer list? As a high achiever we ought to do ten times as much for others as anyone would do for us.

Developing Your High Goal Climbing Planner: An Exercise

An old Oriental proverb says, "A journey of a thousand miles always begins with a single step." Now it's time for you to take that crucial first step in becoming a high achiever: developing your High Goal Climbing Plan. Following is a form that I have used in many seminars to help people develop and organize their own High Goal Climbing Plans. I have filled it in as an example of how it should be used. You may make up one of your own. The important thing is that you develop a complete High Goal Climbing Plan that works for you.

Start by writing the high goal you wish to achieve on the top line. Next, write the first step you can take toward reaching that goal on the line that says "Starting Goal." Then carefully list at least ten progressively higher intermediate goals you must achieve to reach your high goal. Finally, write inside the parentheses the names of the guides who will lead you through every step of your long climb. Be sure to put a date for completion next to your starting goal, each of the intermediate goals, and your high goal.

Make sure that you allow for every stage of preparation, including studying, developing skills, collecting resources, conditioning all three of your personal dimensions, and developing your guide relationships. If you are serious about becoming a high achiever, remember that you must set high goals in every area of responsibility.

Living On The High Goals Cycle

The second tool of the high achiever is the High Goals Cycle. In his book *Living Under Tension*, Harry Emerson Fosdick wrote, "No steam or gas ever drives anything until it is confined. No Niagara is ever turned into light and power until it is funneled. No life ever grows great until it is focused, dedicated, and disciplined."

The High Goals Cycle enables the high achiever to be focused, dedicated, and disciplined and to be free from mass confusion and conformity in our society. By continually rotating around the High Goals Cycle, you can accomplish high goals, not just once in life, but throughout life. It makes no difference whether you are seventeen or seventy, the High Goals Cycle works. It becomes a way of life for the high achiever. There are four components in the High Goals Cycle: dream, study, plan, and act. Each of these components is important, but it is equally important that they be held together synergistically. When each is allowed to do its part, with all working together, these four components

HIGH GOAL: CLIMB MATTERHORN (Alfons. 9/79)

**HIGH GOAL
CLIMBING
PLAN**

Rifflehorn climb (Alfons. 7/79)

Cindy's Okay (Diane Inspiration 6/79)

full marathon 26 mi. (books other runners 6/79)

Grand Teton climb (mountain guide 8/78)

Intermediate Goals

mtn climbing school (instructors 5/78)

13 mi / Mini Marathon (dentist friend 5/78)

10½ miles (3/78)

5 miles (2/78)

3 miles (1/78)

run around block (12/78)

Starting Goal   Guide(s)

enable the high achiever to move continuously toward
higher goals. Let's take a closer look at each one and see
how one affects the other.

1. Dream. A person doesn't become old until his
regrets take the place of his dreams. The high achiever,
using the High Goals Cycle, will never allow this to happen. The high achiever never gets old, he or she just gets
better.

The key to dreaming is visualizing. Human beings
think in terms of images. In order to dream effectively,
the high achiever uses the technique of visualization to
focus precisely on the high goals he or she wants to
reach. Your dreams may include a better job, a higher
income, or a great adventure.

The images you develop program your subconscious
toward achieving them as realities. That is why it's important to have big dreams.

No matter how wild a dream may seem, don't let go

of it. History is full of individuals who become successful by doing what others thought was impossible or impractical. Although you'll make some mistakes and have some unrealistic dreams, don't worry! As James Allen wrote in *As a Man Thinketh*, "He who cherishes a beautiful vision, a lofty ideal in his heart, will one day realize it."

2. *Study.* After you have generated a number of dreamed ideas and high goals, it is time to study resources other than your own mind to generate more ideas and to begin identifying the intermediate steps required for reaching them.

I recommend spending at least half an hour a day studying—using resources other than your own mind. You may want to spend more time when you first start, but if you can average one half hour per day, you'll be amazed at the new and exciting ideas and goals that come into your mind.

Spend your study time flipping through magazines and books in the subject areas of your dreams and ambitions. Cut out pictures and articles related to your goals, and begin to build subject matter and interest files. Frame a picture that represents your high goal and hang it in your office or at home. An interesting aspect of placing a picture of your goal in your office or home is that other people may ask you what it means. When you tell them it is your most important goal, you will be fixing that goal more deeply into your conscious and subconscious mind. The more committed to your high goal you become, the greater the probability of your accomplishing it. Once you've told others about it, you begin to feel that you cannot face them again unless you at least try.

In addition, begin reading about the lives of other successful high achievers in your area of interest, as well as in other areas. Listen to inspirational tapes, seek wise counsel, and plug into the universal power of God's word—the Bible.

3.   Plan. The third component of the High Goal Cycle is to plan. Historian Arnold Toynbee once said, "Apathy can only be overcome by enthusiasm, and enthusiasm can only be aroused by two things: First an ideal which takes the imagination by storm, and second a definite, intelligible plan for carrying that ideal into practice."

The first key to planning is visualizing the *process* of what it will take to reach your high goal. Let your heart and mind work out the details for you. Write them down. Then put them into your interest and goal files and occasionally review them.

The second key in planning is the law of comparative advantage. This law states that high achievers have an economic advantage in one area that can be exploited. For example, if a man is both an excellent typist and an average lawyer, he has a greater comparative economic advantage in practicing law. Likewise, if you own a company and are the chief source of new business for it, you may be violating the law of comparative advantage if you try to keep the books, too. Good bookkeepers and accountants are available, but people who bring in new business are scarce.

In your planning you need to analyze the high goals you have generated in terms of the law of comparative advantage. To give yourself more time for high goal achievement, decide which activities now occupying your time you could give up, delegate to others, or spend less time doing. For example, if your high goal is to write a book while you are working at a full-time job, you're probably going to have to give up some TV viewing, baseball coaching, or other activities. As a high achiever, it is important you manage your time effectively. Don't do jobs that others can do. Delegation is as important in your personal life as it is in your professional life.

4. Act. The hardest part of the High Goals Cycle is taking action toward your high goal. The high achiever can't afford to wait around for an invitation to succeed. That's the way to end up in the "loser's hall of fame" as one of those who had great potential. There comes a time when we have to go for it.

To initiate this action, I use the same technique of visualization that I discussed in the previous "dream" and "plan" sections. It's a little like a mental rehearsal, like projecting in your mind pictures of yourself doing, acting, and succeeding in your high goals. The more realistic your mental pictures, the better. Get the actual sensation of each action: how you feel while doing it. Ingrain this into your conscious and subconscious mind through visualization.

Psychologists have found that mentally acting out the goal-accomplishing process helps make it happen. For example, when I started training and conditioning myself to climb the Matterhorn, as I would run along those long roads, I kept looking down at my feet and, with every step, would say, "One day these feet are going to stand on top of the Matterhorn!" This mental picture helped carry me to the top.

That's the High Goal Cycle. With it, you will move ever upward on life's renewal curve. But never let the intensity of your actions slow down or stop. Keep renewing yourself by using the High Goal Cycle to climb your way to the peak of your reward.

14

Life as a Series of Renewals

Many people who have attended my seminars have told me that the concept of life as a series of renewals was the most important idea communicated during the sessions.

Traditional reasoning has deceived us into thinking of our lives in mechanical terms. We tend to think in terms of growing old and becoming obsolete. Our society's fascination with material possessions undoubtedly influences our thinking. We buy new cars, houses, lawn mowers, clothes, boats. Soon, the new purchases that we wanted so desperately begin to wear out. So we fix them up and they continue to work just fine. A few years later they begin to look old. In another few years, major repair might be necessary. Scratches and dents are quite obvious. Suddenly, our next-door neighbor goes out and buys a new product, and then ours really looks bad, so we feel we need to make a new purchase again.

We tend to think of ourselves in those same mechanical terms. We come into this world brand new and im-

mediately begin to grow and learn. We have high hopes.
But somewhere along life's pathway we begin to wear
down. Some of our hopes get dashed, and our bodies
start to show signs of aging. Gradually, the reality of
our mortality begins to sink in, and we begin to worry
about life's end. Will we be replaced by a new machine
in our work? Will our spouse seek a younger partner?
Will our kids outgrow their need for us? Will we also
end up in the junk pile? How devastating this type of
thinking can be!

High achievers need a long perspective for their lives
and their accomplishments. The high achiever must
view his or her life as a series of renewals. Renewals are
a way of looking at the different periods of our lives.
Those periods require different activities, high goals,
and relationships.

Very little in our society today provides a philosophi-
cal basis for how to live in our later years. The emphasis
is on getting started, not on how to finish. We are bombarded daily with commercials enticing us to look for
the "fountain of youth."

But why not look for the "fountain of age"? The
middle through older years can be a rich, fulfilling time
with as much growth and experimentation as adoles-
cence, and with greater wisdom. We know better what
to take and what to leave behind as we exchange youth
for experience. When Thomas Jefferson was seventy-
two, he was asked by his friend John Adams if he would
go back to the cradle and live his seventy-two years
again. Jefferson's response was that he would gladly
relive the period from age fifty-five to sixty.

Let's begin to change our thinking right now. Life is
not mechanical—it is a series of renewals. Let's look at
life, for a moment, as a series of four periods.

Four Stages of Renewal

The high achiever, like everyone else, goes through the first stage of life, the *education stage*, learning skills and behavior. He or she may or may not excel here. The next stages are where the high achiever becomes separated from the pack. The second stage, the *effectiveness stage*, is where high achievers begin to make their contributions. Achievements mount higher and higher, leading to the third stage, the *consultative stage*. Here, the high achievers have built a reputation for accomplishment, and others eagerly seek their advice and counsel. This stage is not retirement, as it is usually viewed by society, nor is it a stage for being put out to pasture for leisure activity only. It is a rewarding stage for the high achiever who shares the wisdom of experience.

It is in the consultative stage that high achievers become excellent guides. They have done what those who seek their guidance want to do, and they can offer advice that is very useful to younger people.

The fourth and final stage is the *reward stage*, which comes after death. The true high achiever does not want to miss this because it is the ultimate achievement. High achievers do not accept physical death as final. They know they will be held accountable by their Maker, and face a day of reward or punishment after death. High achievers may not fully comprehend life after death, but they do not fear it. They anticipate its eventual arrival and live each day with this stage in mind. Consequently, they age gracefully and thank God for all He has enabled them to accomplish, happily sharing with others what they have learned.

High achievers who make life a series of renewals are like sponges absorbing everything around them. They delight in people, places, and opportunities throughout their lives.

It is possible for high achievers to blend the first three stages throughout their lives so that at any given time they may be learning, doing, and advising.

A Great Example

One of the greatest stories illustrating the concept of life as a series of renewals is the story of Indiana University's swimming coach, James "Doc" Counsilman, who is called "the oldest man in the sea."

At the age of fifty-eight Doc set a world record as the oldest person ever to swim the English Channel. His story of personal triumph began in his youth, when he had the idea of swimming the channel. While he was a student at Ohio State University, he became a breaststroke champion. His ensuing coaching career included twenty consecutive Big Ten championships at Indiana University. He coached the U.S. Olympic swimming team twice and was instrumental in the triumphs of twenty-seven gold medalists.

At a time in life when a record as impressive as his would be enough satisfaction for most men, Doc never forgot his dream of conquering the channel. To him, growing older did not necessarily mean growing softer. At the age of fifty-seven, Doc began preparing to swim the channel, the most challenging body of water a person can cross. He chose mid-September as the target date for his assault on the channel because of the favorable tidal conditions and because the sixty-degree water temperature would be cold enough to discourage sharks.

At 6:13 A.M. on September 14, 1979, Doc slid into the channel waters. He was coated with grease to ward off the cold. He began one of mankind's most classic solo struggles against the forces of nature. Supported by a fully outfitted trawler; assisted by his expert guide, Mike Reid, who had conquered the channel 17 times; and encouraged by his wife Margery, Counsilman moved into his programmed 72 strokes per minute and headed for France.

"Just keep swimming until you get there," Reid urged. Thirteen hours and seventeen minutes after entering the English Channel, Doc emerged victorious on the beach of Wissant, France, about five miles north of his original goal. He staggered a bit upon reaching shore before he recovered his "land legs." He told reporters, "I feel as though I could have gone a couple of more miles." His total swim was measured at 26.5 miles.

Asked if he thought his new record would stand as long as the previous record, 28 years, Doc replied, "I don't believe it will stand long at all as other older people attempt it." In fact, Doc is actively encouraging other older citizens to take off and fulfill their dreams.

Life's Renewal Points

NASA's space experts discovered that there are certain pivotal points in each flight that must be handled correctly so that space vehicles land on their targets. For example, in going to the moon, overcompensation in a midpoint correction can either lead to a rough entry into the moon's atmosphere or to missing the moon's gravity field and beginning an endless ride into outer space.

Undercompensation can result in having to use excess fuel later.

If these admustment points are planned and executed properly, they can be handled with a minimal expenditure of energy. "The most critical factor in making such adjustments is the attitude of the vehicle," said one NASA official.

There are many of these midpoint correction opportunities in the life of the high achiever. Those who recognize and plan for them can use them as renewal points.

Here are examples of renewal points:

- Starting school
- Leaving home to go to college
- Graduating from college
- Getting married
- Moving to a new city
- Having children
- Leaving a job
- Becoming a Christian
- Retiring from our careers
- Graduating from high school
- Entering or leaving military service
- Taking our first real job
- Buying a house
- Completing an early career, like athletics or modeling
- Having our children grow up and leave home

You've probably been through some of those renewal points and maybe some that are not on the list.

Just as in going to the moon, the critical factor in making midpoint corrections is your attitude. If you approach these points with apprehension, look at them as problems, and resist them, they can become traumatic experiences. But if you approach them positively and plan for them, they can launch you into new dimensions of high achievement.

Early in my career with the meat-packing company, I was transferred from Chicago to Louisville. My wife and I moved with the understanding that we would only be there for one year, so we rented an apartment, kept to ourselves, and made our jobs our only outside interest because we viewed this as a temporary situation. But one year stretched into two years, and our move began to take on an air of permanence.

"What do you do when you're not working?" the president, Rod Stephens, asked me one day.

I explained to him that we viewed our stay in Louisville as temporary and hadn't made much effort to establish roots there. We had not joined a church, become involved with the life of the community, or cultivated any deep friendships.

"John," he admonished me, "I want to tell you something that can change the way you live. It's something I've learned by experience. If you stay with this company and continue to climb the ladder, you'll be transferred all over this country. Your life will be much richer if you'll get fully involved with each community as if you are going to be there the rest of your life. You'll find it a lot less painful to break roots than to live without them."

So we decided to try it. We joined a church, got involved in the life of that community, and developed some lasting friendships. And it worked! We soon found ourselves thoroughly enjoying Louisville. Cindy and I now look back at the remainder of the year and a half we spent there as one of the richest experiences of our lives together. From that experience we've learned to live life fully wherever we find ourselves. What a difference that attitude has made!

Getting the most out of life's renewal points includes several key attitudes and actions. First, approach each renewal point positively. Look for the best in every change life brings your way. For example, if you're approaching retirement age, don't view it as being turned out to pasture, accepting a life of passivity. Instead, look for opportunities to become active in ways that have not been possible before. Many people find their retirement years to be their time of greatest joy and usefulness.

Second, take the time to re-evaluate your purpose and goals. Look at how each renewal point affects your life's underlying purpose. Explore how each affects your goals. Make new and progressively higher intermediate goals with each renewal point.

Third, make whatever adjustments are called for. Plan for every problem a renewal point presents, and walk into it with your eyes wide open.

Finally, don't look back. Learn to trust your judgment, experience, and instincts. If you are living by the peak principles of high achievement, you can handle whatever life brings your way.

One of my favorite stories tells of an old man who was sitting beside the railway station in a small midwestern town many years ago.

"I'm looking for a place to live," said a stranger getting off an inbound train. "What kind of town is this?"

"What kind of town are you looking for?" the old man asked.

"Not like the last town I lived in." exclaimed the stranger. "The people there were grouchy, the economy was bad. It was a terrible place!"

"You won't like this town either," replied the old man. "You'll find it's full of grouches, jobs are scarce, and it can be very unpleasant."

Soon, another stranger from the same train approached and asked the same question. When the old man asked what kind of town he was looking for, the second stranger said, "I'd like to find a place like the town I just left. The people there were nice, opportunities abounded, and the weather was delightful."

"Oh, then you'll like this town," said the old man. "The people are nice, there are plenty of jobs, and the weather is beautiful."

A young man who had overheard the conversation asked the old man to explain why he had given such different answers to the two men. "I know you to be a truthful man," he said, "yet you described this town like two different places."

"Son," said the old man, "People find what they're looking for in any town."

That's the way it is with life's renewal points. They can either be exciting adventures or traumatic experiences—the only variable is your attitude toward them.

15

Kilimanjaro

As the heavens are higher than
   the earth,
so are My ways higher than
your ways
and My thoughts than your
thoughts.
                              —Isa. 55:9

Kilimanjaro stands alone as Africa's "mountain of greatness."

"As wide as all the world, great, high, and unbelievably white in the sun was the square top of Kilimanjaro." This is how Ernest Hemingway captured its majesty in *"The Snows of Kilimanjaro.*

In January 1982, Cindy and I flew to Tanzania, Africa, to assault this magnificent expression of God's creativity.

Why Kilimanjaro?

When Cindy and I first announced that we were going to climb this 19,340-foot latent volcano, which on a clear day can be seen for more than 100 miles, our family, friends, and associates had only one question: Why?

Cindy's reasons were quite simple. First, she believed it would enrich our marriage if we shared lofty and deeply spiritual achievements. Secondly, she wanted to prove herself after her Grand Teton experience.

I shared Cindy's first reason for wanting to climb Kilimanjaro, but other than that, the question of why Kilimanjaro was not easy for me to answer. In fact, it raised a host of other questions and considerations. As a mountaineer I had nothing to prove. And I had many accomplishments in my business, my community, and in speaking circles throughout America. Moreover, I had a lot to lose if I failed in my attempt to climb Mount Kilimanjaro. As a professional speaker and seminar leader, how could I face another audience and talk to them about mountain climbing and high achievement if I had been forced to quit before I reached the top? Why not settle for past glories, and continue developing myself in my other areas of achievement?

Climbing Kilimanjaro was a dream I had cherished since reading Hemingway's *The Snows of Kilimanjaro* as a young man. Both my fascination with mountains and my opinion that Kilimanjaro is one of the greatest mountains lured me to it. It stands there like a giant sentinel dominating that entire region. So startling is this snow-covered mountain that when it was first discovered in 1848 by Johannes Redmann it took thirteen years to convince Europeans that such a phenomenon as a four-mile-high mountain covered with snow could exist only three degrees from the Equator.

Perhaps the lure of Kilimanjaro is its desolation, so great that nothing can live on its pinnacle for long without an outside support system. The extremely high altitude, thin air, and temperatures ranging from 15° to 105° by day offer ultimate sensations in mental and physical stimulation. Maybe I had become so geared to goal-oriented activities, which stretch my imagination to reach for my full potential, that I could not resist such a challenge.

These reasons, combined with the possibility that Cindy and I could visit our church missionaries in the region and enjoy spiritual growth together made the urge overpowering. Whatever the reasons, when we arrived we knew that we wanted to be nowhere else.

A Whole New Ball Game

For me, Kilimanjaro was a whole new ball game. The climb is not difficult in technical mountaineering terms. It has none of the shoulders and ledges of the Matterhorn. You don't need crampons, and there is no dangling from a rope a mile above the glacier floor. I've heard that climbing Kilimanjaro is a little like "clambering up nine Empire State Buildings laid end to end on an incline, or like mounting a staircase more than two miles long." However, at 15,500 feet, where the final assault begins, there is little more than half the oxygen you'll find at sea level. The thin air, extreme temperatures, threatening winds and snows, and physical impact of rapidly changing altitudes can reduce a man in his prime to resembling a sick and feeble old man very quickly.

The climb itself takes five days and four nights, covering more than seventy miles. On the final assault, the climbing is made more difficult by the scree (lava dust) that covers the mountain's peak. It's a little like slogging up a steep hill in knee-deep mud. At sea level such physical exertion is very demanding, but at extremely high altitudes it's murder!

There are other dangers that can be life-threatening. Dehydration is a constant danger and breathing becomes extremely labored. That combination of conditions sometimes results in death even to physically fit climbers through a condition called pulmonary edema —your lungs fill up with fluids, and you essentially drown.

Every movement you make on Kilimanjaro becomes extremely difficult and exhausting. One of the best ways to discover just how strenuous activities become is to notice how difficult routine functions are. For example, at sea level it is a simple matter to wash your hands before eating. At 15,500 feet it suddenly becomes a challenging exercise. At night, you sleep lightly, often experiencing wild dreams. Rolling over in your sleeping bag becomes a major chore. Any sudden movement results in a sharp, penetrating headache. The overwhelming natural urge is to lie down, rest, and drift off into sleep, yet sleep won't come.

Nausea and diarrhea are constant problems. It is not at all uncommon to be ravenously hungry but to be sickened by the very thought of food. In short, high-altitude climbing puts strain on the body, mind, and spirit that are not known in any other area of human activity.

"Polé Polé"

Miss Lanny, our outfitter, four-time Kilimanjaro climber, offered us some great advice in Swahili. She said we should go "polé polé"—that's "slowly slowly."

At first, that advice seemed overly cautious, or meant for those people who were not as well conditioned as Cindy and I were. But it didn't take us long to realize the value of her guidance. Halfway up, when we saw a couple of climbers being brought down on wheeled stretchers, suffering from pulmonary edema resulting from climbing too rapidly, we were inspired to go "polé polé."

Climbing Kilimanjaro was something Cindy and I expected to be a spiritual experience. We knew that expectation was to become reality when we discovered that one of our two guides was named Moses. What better name for a guide to take you to the top of a mountain? Our other guide was named Good Luck. With Moses and Good Luck to guide us, we couldn't miss!

By the end of the second day it had become obvious that everything we had been led to believe about Kilimanjaro was true. She is truly Africa's great mountain, and one of the most extraordinary displays of God's handiwork on the face of the earth.

At 14,000 feet, the surroundings become very stark, rather like the pictures beamed back from the moon by NASA's astronauts. There are no trees, no vegetation, no animals, and very little air. The ominous peak looks almost clear enough to reach out and touch, but you know it is still a long way off. Every step requires a major expenditure of energy, a great exercise of will.

At 15,500 feet we were ready to make our final assault on the snow-covered crest of Mount Kilimanjaro. Here we would leave our porters and burden-bearers and make the remainder of the climb with only our two guides. Moses and Good Luck had advised that we should leave in the middle of the night in order to climb to the summit, spend a little time there, and make it back down to Horombo Hut at the 12,500-foot level, by nightfall. That way we wouldn't have to spend another night at the 15,500-foot level where the altitude is so oppressive.

The Final Assault

At 1:40 A.M., the moon was shining brightly. Two-thirds full, it lit up the whole mountain—an incredible sight. For the next five hours we slogged through the increasingly thick scree. Without a doubt, this was the most physically exhausting five-hour period of my life. It felt as if each of my feet weighed a ton, and putting one foot ahead of the other drew all my concentration. I was impressed that Cindy persisted too despite sickness, fatigue, and the extreme difficulty of climbing.

Just as the sun broke over the horizon, we reached the summit—19,340 above sea level. The sky was crystal clear. The silence was complete. There was no wind, no sound at all—total silence. It was as if someone had plugged our ears. Moses said he'd never seen it like this.

The spiritual experience Cindy and I had expected at this lofty point proved to be everything we had hoped for. Someone had placed a plaque at the highest point on the peak, which read: "All the earth worships Thee: they sing praises to Thee, sing praises to Thy name." For us, that quotation from Psalms confirmed that others had shared our awareness of God's love and power at this high and majestic place. The sensations I vividly remember from the short time we spent on the summit were the sound of the blood pounding within my head and the sight of the whole world beneath me. It was the greatest experience of communion with God that I could ever imagine.

But it was time to start the long trek downward, which I did not relish at all. I could just imagine the beating we would suffer climbing down all the winding paths we'd followed to the top. I could imagine slogging our way back down through the exhausting scree, fighting it every step of the way. Much to my surprise, Moses grabbed Cindy by the arm, locked their arms together and said, "Follow me!" He threw his feet straight out in front of him, sailed about four feet through the air, then sank his feet into the soft scree beneath him. Cindy followed right along. Time after time they jumped four feet out and down at a clip. I followed suit, and straight down we went at a tremendous pace. So fast was that descent, it took us only one hour to cover the same distance we had spent five hours climbing earlier that morning. In no time at all we reached the Kibo Hut, rested for half an hour, ate a quick lunch, and then began our trek down to Horombo Hut to spend the night. The next day, after the remaining twenty-two mile hike downhill, we reached the park entrance.

We were near exhaustion, sore all over, but elated with joy. Together, Cindy and I had climbed the great mountain I had dreamed about as a boy.

Where to Now?

What's the next high goal for Cindy and me? We'll keep climbing onward, since we have discovered the tremendous exhilaration that comes from living on the High Goals Cycle, sharing high achievements together, and constantly renewing our high goals in life.

I hope that this book has helped inspire you to set high goals and become a high achiever.

When I end my seminars, I always close by saying, "May you have a good climb in your life and may you climb from peak to peak to The Peak, the Summit with God!"

This is my prayer for you: May all your goals be high goals, all your failures glorious failures, and all your achievements high achievements!

Epilogue:

A Personal Story

Ever since I began climbing some of the greatest mountains of the world, I have often received invitations to speak to people in various business and church groups. My subject has been to help people reach heights in their lives that they never dreamed possible. Inevitably, a few individuals will come up after such presentations and ask me questions such as, Why are *you* so excited about life? Or, What makes *your* life seem so motivated? I wasn't always like this, I explain. While on my first few mountain climbs, I learned the importance of climbing fully equipped. Everywhere I climbed, I hired expert guides, bearers and outfitters. I put all my trust and confidence in them and never worried. This freed me to concentrate on climbing higher—higher than I could have ever climbed by myself.

Shortly after returning from climbing the Matterhorn, God dramatically changed my life. I felt a strong pull to climb fully equipped with Him, too. But why? I didn't need God—I had a fulfilling career, and I was building a successful business on my own. I didn't need God for material wealth. I owned a fashionable home and two new cars, had toured all around the world, and had good health. I didn't need God to have a wonderful family. I had married a lovely woman and was raising two well-behaved children. I didn't need God. I was doing well on my own.

But I also knew one other thing. Even though my life looked full, I knew that under the surface I didn't have anything. There was a persistent emptiness, a void, a fear, and an agony that was tearing me apart inside. It wouldn't go away. It just grew worse, the more success I achieved. But as I read about the lives of others—great writers, actors, famous or everyday people—I found I wasn't unusual. They, too, felt this way. Was I trying to climb through life partially equipped?

At the age of thirty-three, I decided to climb fully equipped with God and tap into His motivational power. This brought me face-to-face with the question, Who is Jesus Christ? Jesus made an astounding claim: "I am the way, the truth, and the life. No man cometh unto the Father, but by me." (John 14:6) "I and my Father are one." (John 10:30) I wrestled with the inescapable fact that either Jesus was who He claimed to be, or He was the biggest liar, fraud, or lunatic in history. Which was it?

The happiest day of my life was the day in November, 1979, when I finally realized that Jesus Christ is who He says He is. His life, death, and resurrection are some of the best-attested facts in all history. Several hundred specific and general prophecies made over more than a thousand-year period were fulfilled in Him. Those of us who have studied these prophecies in depth can confirm His credentials as the Messiah. No person other than Jesus, living or dead, could have fulfilled even one or two of these prophecies. Jesus said about Himself, "And ye shall know the truth, and truth shall make you free." (John 8:32) He also said, "I am come that they might have life, and that they might have it *more* abundantly." (John 10:10) He wants to motivate you and me, to show us how to have that more abundant way of living.

I prayed and invited Jesus Christ to come into my life as both my Lord and my Savior. As a boy, I had joined a church. But I wasn't sure I knew Jesus personally, at least not as my Lord. Later I resisted giving Him complete control of my life, my business, my money, my family, my future, and my bad habits until that November day. Since then, I've discovered what living fully equipped is all about. Jesus Christ is the switch that completes the connection between man and God. He made God's unlimited motivational power available to me. He started to work in my life just as he had promised: "Call unto me and I will answer thee, and show thee great and mighty things which thou knowest not." (Jeremiah 33:3)

He started a process of guiding and motivating me to new heights of creativity and success. He replaced my inner struggles with a sense of peace and relaxation. He inspired me to accomplishments greater than I ever could have imagined on my own.

I found that my desire to know God and His spiritual truths increased noticeably. I started attending Bible studies and listening with renewed interest to God's Word. Our entire family grew spiritually. We transferred our membership to a Christ-centered, Bible-oriented church. The changes didn't stop there.

In my business, He brought me a new idea. Instead of traveling around the Midwest, banging on factory doors as an outside cleaning contractor trying to get work away from in-house employees, why not equip, train, and direct the in-house people to do a more efficient job? Our business (God's and mine) quadrupled and is still growing.

Furthermore, God began providing me with invitations to speak to business and church groups. As I shared the mountain-climbing insights and motivational messages He had given me, I received more and more invitations. My speaking engagements developed into full-day seminars.

In my teaching, He helped me put together an evangelism course called "Effective Witnessing" for our church. It's exciting to see how He's extending Himself through me.

Last, God is using me to lead other people to Jesus Christ and to that more abundant life.

Yes, I still have problems in my daily life, because I'm human—I'm not perfect. However, my life has taken on a new and thrilling dimension. Every day I'm discovering new reasons why living life to its fullest can be achieved only when you are climbing fully equipped in Christ. Likewise, the greatest motivational truths are God's laws[1] that govern our relationship with Him:

1. God loves you and offers a wonderful plan for your life. (John 3:16 and John 10:10)
2. Man is sinful and separated from God. Therefore, you cannot know and experience God's love and plan for your life. (Rom. 3:23 and Rom. 6:23)
3. Jesus Christ is God's only provision for man's sin. Through Him you can know and experience God's love and plan for your life. (Rom. 5:8 and John 14:6)

4. You must individually confess and receive Jesus Christ to be your Savior and Lord. Then, you can know and experience God's love and plan for your life. (John 1:12, Eph. 2:8-9, and Rev. 3:20)

The most important decision I have ever made was my commitment to Jesus Christ. Just as I did a few years ago, you can receive Christ right now by faith through prayer. The following is a suggested prayer:

Lord Jesus, I need You. Thank You for dying on the cross for my sins. I open the door of my life and receive You as my Savior and Lord. Thank You for forgiving my sins and giving me eternal life. Take control of the throne of my life. Make me the kind of person You want me to be. Amen.[1]